The Arnold and Caroline Rose Monograph Series
of the American Sociological Association

Middle Start

An experiment in the educational enrichment
of young adolescents

Other books in the series

James A. Geschwender: *Class, Race, and Worker Insurgency: The League of Revolutionary Black Workers*

Paul Ritterband: *Education, Employment, and Migration: Israel in Comparative Perspective*

John Low-Beer: *Protest and Participation: The New Working Class in Italy*

Volumes previously published by the American Sociological Association

Michael Schwartz and Sheldon Stryker: *Deviance, Selves and Others*

Robert M. Hauser: *Socioeconomic Background and Educational Performance*

Morris Rosenberg and Roberta G. Simmons: *Black and White Self-Esteem: The Urban School Child*

Chad Gordon: *Looking Ahead: Self-Conceptions, Race and Family as Determinants of Adolescent Orientation to Achievement*

Anthony M. Orum: *Black Students in Protest: A Study of the Origins of the Black Student Movement*

Ruth M. Gasson, Archibald O. Haller, and William H. Sewell: *Attitudes and Facilitation in the Attainment of Status*

Sheila R. Klatzky: *Patterns of Contact with Relatives*

Herman Turk: *Interorganizational Activation in Urban Communities: Deductions from the Concept of System*

John DeLamater: *The Study of Political Commitment*

Alan C. Kerckhoff: *Ambition and Attainment: A Study of Four Samples of American Boys*

Scott McNall: *The Greek Peasant*

Lowell L. Hargens: *Patterns of Scientific Research: A Comparative Analysis of Research in Three Scientific Fields*

Charles Hirschman: *Ethnic Stratification in Peninsular Malaysia*

Middle Start

An experiment in the educational enrichment
of young adolescents

J. Milton Yinger

Professor of Sociology and Anthropology
Oberlin College

Kiyoshi Ikeda

Professor of Sociology
University of Hawaii

Frank Laycock

Professor of Education
Oberlin College

Stephen J. Cutler

Associate Professor of Sociology and Anthropology
Oberlin College

Cambridge University Press

Cambridge

London   New York   Melbourne

371.967
M 627

Published by the Syndics of the Cambridge University Press
The Pitt Building, Trumpington Street, Cambridge CB2 1RP
Bentley House, 200 Euston Road, London NW1 2DB
32 East 57th Street, New York, NY 10022, USA
296 Beaconsfield Parade, Middle Park, Melbourne 3206, Australia

First published 1977

Printed in the United States of America
Typeset by Telecki Publishing Services, Yonkers, New York
Printed and bound by the Murray Printing Company, Westford, Massachusetts

Library of Congress Cataloging in Publication Data

Main entry under title:

Middle start.

(The Arnold and Caroline Rose monograph series of the
American Sociological Association)

Bibliography: p.

Includes index.

    1. Socially handicapped children — Education (Secondary) — United States.
2. Vacation schools — United States. I. Yinger, John Milton.
II. Series: The Arnold and Caroline Rose monograph series in sociology.
LC4091.M48 371.9'67 76-47186
ISBN 0 521 21604 4 hard covers
ISBN 0 521 29207 7 paperback

Contents

Appendixes

Tables

Preface

We are living in a day when aspirations are rising among all segments of the population, but most dramatically among the economically disadvantaged. And once the possibilities of a new life are made visible to all, there is no way, as David Riesman once put it, to ration dreams. It is also a time when the enormous complexities and difficulties of social engineering are becoming increasingly apparent. The disparity between the rate of change in aspiration and the rate at which obstacles are being removed has no doubt contributed to the tensions of a heterogeneous, urban society. Confronted with these tensions, one is tempted to indulge in utopian dreams or, alternatively, to resort to cynicism — or to vacillate between them. But neither utopianism, ungrounded in the social realities, nor cynicism, disarming effort, holds much promise of realizing newly formed aspirations. The research reported here supports a quiet confidence that we can, by taking thought, make some progress toward solution of the problem.

Interested in both the structure of opportunity and the processes of socialization, we asked if an imaginative program to help educate and stimulate thirteen- and fourteen-year-olds could eliminate or reduce educational deficits resulting from economic deprivation in the family and the community. (Such deficits, we believed, were more closely associated with the structure of opportunities than with individual characteristics.) To find an answer, we designed a field experiment in which we recognized the need for varied forms of intervention and for controlled observation, and analyzed its impact over a seven-year period. We report in the role of research workers, but it will be clear that we have a strong interest in the program. Although we were not directly involved in its administration, we did help to design it and we sought to make it successful. Readers can decide better than we whether our active interest in it — and in the critical problems it addressed — has affected our analysis.

We are indebted to scores of people, more than in most studies of this scope. School personnel in five cities, administrators and teachers in the program, colleagues in many parts of the country, college counselors, interviewers, parents, and the students themselves, along with research assistants over the seven years, *all* made important contributions. At the risk of omitting the names of some who have been particularly helpful, we must thank at least the following: Professor John Antes, now of the University of Wisconsin, and Mr. William Parker, now at the Educational Testing Service, who ably served as directors of the program; Dr. Alva Dittrick, Mr. Julius Dix, Mrs. Nancy Fields, Dr. Margaret Fleming, Miss Ella Johnson, Dr. Samuel Shepard, and Mr. Donald Swift, officials in the school districts with which we worked, all of whom gave staunch support to both the program and the research.

Professor Donald T. Campbell and Professor William H. Sewell made valuable suggestions. Mrs. Nancy Aschaffenburg, who was on the staff for the whole period of the research, kept the massive data in order; when no one else could find a necessary piece of information, she could go right to it. Robert Kaufman skillfully executed our estimation procedures by computer. We could not have wished for better colleagues than the Oberlin College students who served as coders and computer assistants, in particular Pem Buck, Mary Jean Galloway, Janet Grigsby, Mary Johnson Guttmacher, Peter Johnson, Kent McClelland, Peter Reeves, Margaret Rhile, Barbara Greer Williams, and Robert Kaufman. Several of them, especially Robert Kaufman, could well be regarded as coauthors. Ida Simpson and her editorial board on the Rose Monograph Series of the American Sociological Association were extraordinarily helpful in their comments and suggestions. The manuscript has been improved in many ways by the fine hand of Helen Hughes.

Estelle Berman, Debby Lirette, Suzie Sanders, and Betty Berman and her staff, particularly Linda Posey, typed various versions of the manuscript with skill and patience. We are grateful for their talents at deciphering polygraphic scribbling.

The Rockefeller Foundation was generous in its support of the summer and follow-up program. We believe this report shows that they invested wisely in the hundreds of young people involved. Essential to the study was the funding of the first five years of our research by the Bureau of Research, Office of Education of the United States Department of Health, Education, and Welfare. (Project N. 5-0703; Grant No. 0E 6-

10-255.) Finally, our thanks go to Oberlin College for furnishing — with little regard to the cost — facilities, research space, computer time, and a most stimulating environment.

J. Milton Yinger
Kiyoshi Ikeda
Frank Laycock
Stephen J. Cutler

Oberlin, Ohio
January, 1977

1. The sources of academic achievement: theoretical perspective

Are educational quality and educational equality essential to an open society? If so, can they be attained directly by attention to training; or are they primarily dependent variables, reflecting home and community environment? Are patterns of language and perception, motives to learn, and basic skills set at such an early age that kindergarten is already too late; or are there possibilities for growth at every age, albeit of different kinds and degrees?

During the last decade, such questions have attracted the attention of many scholars and stimulated many public and private programs of action. For example, over ten years ago, in 1965, the United States embarked on an educational enterprise designed to reduce the disadvantages some children carried with them as they entered school: "Head Start," which rapidly became a major project. In 1975 it enrolled 350,000 children, most of whom were in full-year programs, and operated on a budget of $392 million, which Congress renewed for three years.

Somewhat earlier, in 1963, we were asking ourselves whether early adolescence was a strategic time to effect significant changes in educational motivation and performance. We shared the generally held view that inspired Head Start: "the earlier the better"; but we did not believe that attention to the early years would eliminate the need of attention to later years, for we thought the problems differed according to the period of life. This point is well made in a recent monograph on programs of educational intervention in early adolescence:

older children may still have serious basic skills deficiencies despite earlier exposure to special programs if, at the time of that exposure, they were not cognitively ready to gain the maximum benefit from it. Studies by Kagan, Piaget, Elkind and Moore suggest that the rate at which certain cognitive capacities develop is influenced by individual and cultural factors. Thus the children of low income, minority families who form the target group of compensatory education programs, may develop the particular set of skills needed for school learning more slowly than do upper income

1

children. Therefore, not all such children will be able to gain full benefit from even well-designed and generally effective early programs. (Larson and Dittmann, 1975: 4)

Research on issues related to compensatory education has been influenced by school integration and the opposition to it, the increasing importance of education to an urban society, the growing interest in equal opportunity, and other national trends. A variety of sophisticated methods have been used in this research: surveys of large populations have been designed to isolate precisely the factors in individual, family, and community life that keep pupils in school and encourage high achievement.[1] One group of studies examined school integration as it relates to individual and group background, on the one hand, and to school performance on the other.[2] Another series assessed programs specifically designed to help minority children to do better in school.[3] Most of this research is *ex post facto*; seldom is there a control group. As a result the conclusions must be and generally have been stated cautiously.

We report here a field experiment, with carefully selected experimental and control groups, designed to show whether a relatively minor school experience — when judged against all the pressures on academic performance — would have a significant effect on children in the middle years of schooling. The main stimulus was a six-week summer program on a college campus, followed by a modest series of related activities during the succeeding five years. We measured the possible effects of these experiences as indicated by persistence in school, grades and achievement test scores, and the quality of the schools or programs entered after the seventh grade. Our theoretical perspective, of course, determined the independent variables and the methods by which we examined their cumulative effect and their interaction.

Approaches to the study of human behavior

Explanations of human behavior follow waves of style. Today there is some resurgence of the belief that man's capacity for aggression evolves largely from his biological inheritance.[4] Some studies emphasize the biological base of intelligence, concentrating upon individual and racial differences.[5] No one, to our knowledge, denies the influence of experience and opportunity. A number of authors do affirm, however, that most of the variation in intelligence can be accounted for by hereditary factors. Other studies examine the impact of experience, but from a classic or modified Freudian perspective that takes into account only the earliest years when, so some argue, a rich and flexible or a constricting lingual screen is formed, motivation and a sense of self that either support or inhibit intelligence and confidence develop, and levels of nutrition and health either promote development or leave a permanent deficit.[6]

On the other hand, many beliefs, theories, and policies promote the view that experience and opportunity continue to work beyond earliest childhood. Cultural resources, more than genes, set a ceiling on intelligence (Faris, 1961; Hunt in Deutsch, Katz, and Jensen, 1968: chap. 8). Developing a concept of "collective ability," Robert Faris reaffirms the importance of the super-organic influence on human creativity and accomplishment: "to an important degree, a society generates its level of ability . . . the upper limit is unknown and distant . . . the processes of generation of ability are potentially subject to intentional control." The level of ability is influenced, not only by society's funded knowledge but by the distribution of stimuli, the availability of models, the changes that breach constricting "aspiration boundaries." "Few persons can summon their maximum effort against what they conceive to be an absolute impossibility, but their powers may be released if they are shown, by the example of achievement by a person they view to be comparable, that the thing can be done." (Faris, 1961:841.) Implicitly if not explicitly agreeing, the federal government supported Head Start programs for three to five-year-olds and Upward Bound programs for adolescents, in the belief that campaigns such as these will identify and stimulate unused capacities. So, too, colleges and universities now enroll students who do not meet what used to be minimum standards, in the hope that the stimulus of college may be able to reduce the deficits of the first eighteen years.

Those who stress environment do not usually deny the importance of inheritance or the impact of the earliest years. Some psychological behaviorists and sociological structuralists, to be sure, give major attention to external stimuli; but there are few today who overlook, at least in their theoretical statements, the full range of influences on behavior. Among those who argue the case for external forces, however, there is important disagreement on whether the shared norms and values of cultures and subcultures are critical; whether, for example, if two groups differ in educational aspirations and performance, the differences indicate cultural contrast. This point of view is developed most fully by those who employ the concept of a "culture of poverty," the phrase by which they refer to norms and values that in their judgment, give traditional support to poverty as a way of life.[7] It is not simply a matter of low income. Lewis argues that many people in the world are very poor without feeling the hostility to the dominant institutions, the fatalism, and the feelings of helplessness and inferiority that characterize the culture of poverty. The culture of poverty "is a culture in the traditional anthropological sense in that it provides human beings with a design for living, with a ready-made set of solutions for human problems, and so serves a significant adaptive function" (Lewis, 1966: 9).

Other scholars — we shall call them "structuralists" in contrast to the "culturalists" — believe that differences in aspiration and school performance (along with economic, familial, and other differences) come primarily from the structure of opportunities. On the one hand, they argue that values and aspirations are shared throughout a society and across status levels; on the other hand, they stress the great differences in access to resources and opportunities. The culture of poverty, in their view, is a secondary set of norms, a series of painful adjustments to difficult conditions, a "value stretch" by which those in poverty try to deal with limited opportunity, crushed self-esteem, discrimination, and other burdens (Rodman, 1963). As Lee Rainwater puts it, the poor, faced with enormous obstacles when they try to "play the games" of the dominant society, develop their own games, which are to some degree passed along in the socialization process. With specific reference to black Americans, he writes: "The substitute adaptations of each generation condition the possibilities subsequent generations have of adapting in terms of the requirements of the normative games. . . . Nevertheless, in the American context at least it is clear that each generation of Negroes has a strong desire to be able to perform successfully in terms of the norms of the larger society and makes efforts in this direction" (1970: 143).

In the area of our interest, educational plans and performance vary widely among status groups, so the structuralists argue, because of differential opportunities, not because of differential talent or varying cultural support.[8] From this point of view, it follows that sensitive high school counseling, GI Bills or other financial subsidies, the existence of community colleges within commuting distance, and the like, all close the gap between educational aspirations and realistic expectations among the less advantaged.[9]

Clearly, important policy questions are involved in this debate. To the extent that authors such as Oscar Lewis (1966) and Edward Banfield (1968, 1974) are right, elimination of poverty (and, by extension, of educational disadvantage) may do little to abolish the culture of poverty. To the extent that the structuralists are right — and we think the evidence supports them more strongly — the first need, if cycles of poverty and poor educational performance are to be broken, is to alter the social reality, the opportunity system. Efforts to convert the disadvantaged to a new culture or to resocialize them to a different set of values are likely to fail in the absence of new opportunities, realistically available and fully perceived. This is not to say, however, that normative systems adapted to poverty, and individual tendencies that express and help to perpetuate them, do not play a part in the total pattern of causes. Culture and character do not merely reflect the social structure: they strongly influence perception of and response to changes in the structure of opportunities. Although the first requisite in strategies of change is the opening up of opportunities, eventually group norms and individual tendencies must also change. Opportunities are never absolute; they are relative to the attitudes, skills, and perceptions of those who experience them, and to the cultural norms and values through which they are interpreted.

For many of those in poverty a powerful combination of structural and cultural factors is connected with racial discrimination. The causes of poverty, as Duncan has forcefully documented, are by no means identical in the case of Blacks and Whites in the United States (1969: chap. 4). He estimates, for example, that at least one-third of the income gap cannot be accounted for by differences in education, family background, number of siblings, or ability. That one-third is the cost of being a Negro (as of 1962 in the United States). Clearly no simple explanation based on a subculture of poverty is adequate.

To what degree can these approaches be reconciled?

Such complexity, and such diverse interpretations of it, call for a pragmatic attitude, and not too tight a hold on theoretical premises. We sought to find by research which elements in the cycle of causation can best be controlled. We believe it is more important to seek ways to develop the unused capacities in all human beings than to debate how existing circumstances determine the present range of variation in abilities.

We did not start our research, however, lacking judgments and assumptions about the sources of talent and of the factors that promote or inhibit educational achievement. To some degree, we share each of the perspectives mentioned above. We believe that any complete statement must take account of four orders of phenomena: biological factors, early learning, subcultural and cultural influences, and the structure of opportunities; that attention to each of these factors must be significantly qualified, and they must then all be brought into one theoretical system that takes full account of their interdependence. To comment briefly on these points:

First, it appears to us that inheritance does produce some range in human capacities but that this assumption requires two qualifications:

(1) There is no evidence that the range of inherited capacity varies significantly among races. Rather, group variations in measured intelligence reflect the skills tested, the measuring instruments, and the patterns of experience and opportunity.[10] We shall not explore, nor even cite, the vast literature on this subject (but see Simpson and Yinger, 1972: 50—6 and 203—4). To generalize about group differences without full equation of nutrition, stimulus deprivation, experience of discrimination, test conditions, and general environmental support is to rest conclusions on a weak foundation. We believe that the study of intelligence is on much sounder ground when it examines the organism—environment transactions.

(2) Socially shared knowledge and methods of training, more than inheritance, set the ceiling on intelligence. Average men today can understand aspects of the natural world that once baffled geniuses, because, as Newton said, we stand on the shoulders of giants. It is far more important to improve methods of training that lift the base of socially shared knowledge than to dwell on the range of inherited differences.

Second, we recognize the importance of poor stimulation, ego-strength, and nutrition during the early years. This point must also be qualified:

(1) The importance of early life can be exaggerated, because those who are deprived in infancy are usually those who are deprived later as well. We cannot attribute poor motivation or talent to childhood experiences without controlling the reinforcing effects of later experience. (We hope that our research will make some contribution to this problem.)

(2) The importance given to the first few years is not intrinsic to

them, but may be merely a reflection of the present state of our knowledge. We may learn to prevent or overcome nutritional deficits, to reverse or redirect motivation. The evidence is reasonably good that, at the present time, severe protein-calorie deficiencies during the first year of life impair mental development, while moderate malnutrition in later infancy seems to have effects that are reversible. In either case, the deficiencies and the knowledge or lack of knowledge to eliminate them are all part of a socio-cultural system; they are not simply biological facts to be taken as given (Kallen, 1973; Montagu, 1972).

Third, recent research on cultural influences has illuminated their involvement in education. Instead of assuming that American values uniformly support education, we must study their range carefully. Here again, however, the contribution of a particular orientation — in this instance, to cultural variation — is greatest if its limitations are recognized. The study of cultural factors in education must begin with two qualifications:

(1) Culture is not simply an independent variable, causing behavior in a given environment, separately or in conjunction with other factors. Culture itself develops and changes. From one perspective, as already noted, it is a group's adjustment mechanism, one that must be studied in the lives of particular people in particular circumstances (Ball, 1968; Parker and Kleiner, 1970; Rodman, 1963).

(2) In complex societies such as the United States, a wide variety of cultural influences bear on education, only some of which are effective in a particular context (for an analogous point referring to delinquency, see Matza and Sykes, 1961).

Fourth, the opportunities and surrounding stimuli are important in every individual's education, just as they are in his work, politics, and religion. The social structure, as the term is used here, is built of small-scale, personal encounters, broader reference groups of significant others, and the impersonal resources of local and national institutions. Together they make up the opportunities open to any individual. Regardless of personal capacities or the strong cultural value placed on education, the individual's attainment will be limited in the absence of strong structural supports. This proposition must also be qualified:

(1) Individuals respond differently to the same opportunities. That is, changes in opportunity are not enough, in themselves, to guarantee changes in behavior. Individual tendencies and social encouragement are involved. What is an opportunity to one person is an impossible

dream, a threat, or a hoax to another with different tendencies. Interaction effects, as well as the additive effects of separate factors, are crucial.

(2) Subsocieties with somewhat different values and norms also vary in how well they stimulate their members to take advantage of opportunities. If it is unwise to explain behavioral differences between classes by culture alone, it is equally unwise to overlook the fact that societies and groups within them evaluate education differently. Persons of equal talent, facing equal opportunities, will respond differently if their cultural supports vary.

The field theoretical approach

An adequate theory must combine the biological, psychological, cultural, and structural influences on education. We shall not work out such a theory here.[11] But we shall illustrate how it might restate questions related to education and educational attainment. One of the postulates of field theory is that all four influences on behavior must be taken into account, because behavior is the cumulative effect of them; indeed, is often a *product* of their interaction. In the latter case, an activity cannot occur if any one of the four influences is lacking. A corollary is that efforts to improve educational performance are most likely to be successful when several factors are strengthened, since biological, cultural, structural, and psychological influences *combine* to produce a given outcome. That outcome would not occur without all the factors, but the weights assigned to each, under various conditions, need empirical verification. We would posit that, were the data rich enough and the mode of analysis powerful enough, interaction effects would emerge from analysis; nevertheless, this is not necessarily so in any given piece of research. In many systematic empirical studies, total effects have been shown to be composed of both main effects and interactive effects, depending on the statistical tools used.[12]

Let us put the argument for a product model in simple mathematical terms, using fictitious numbers. Assume that a given level of education is a function of inherited capacity, learned skills and motives, cultural definitions of appropriate behavior, and structural opportunities. Assume further that each factor can have a support score ranging from 0 to 10. Now compare two individuals of the same capacity but differing on the other three factors. Their education, the product of all four

Table 1.1. *A field theoretical model of educational performance*

	Inherited capacity	Learned motives and tendencies	Cultural support	Structural support	Product score
Individual *A*	5	5	5	5	625
Individual *B*	5	2	2	2	40

factors, would be sharply different, as seen in the multiplicative model (Table 1.1). If the statement in Table 1.1 is correct, Individual *B* is educationally deprived, and the modification of only one factor cannot help significantly. If some experience should strongly increase *B*'s motives and skills (to a score of 8, say), while the cultural and structural supports remain weak, then in a strictly multiplicative model there is some improvement ($5 \times 8 \times 2 \times 2 = 160$); but *B* still will fall seriously behind Individual *A*, who has equal capacity and poorer motivation, but substantially stronger cultural and structural supports.

In another sense, the simple mathematical model in Table 1.1 indicates that no chain is stronger than its weakest link. We get the largest *product* of four factors that add up to 20 with $5 \times 5 \times 5 \times 5$, the lowest (if zeros are excluded) by combining two nines and two ones. If our interpretation is correct, wise educational policy deals with all possible factors. Theories that emphasize one factor not only are less powerful analytic tools, but they are less useful guides to community action than are multifactor theories. An extraordinarily low score on one factor is likely to mean that compensatory efforts aimed at related factors can have only moderate effect.

We can get an index of the relative influence of "opportunity" effects and of "capacity" effects on education by reexamining the data in Sewell and Shah's study (1967) of a sample of Wisconsin males. In a series of papers Sewell and his colleagues sought the factors that determine who is likely to graduate from college. Effects of opportunity stem from the family's socioeconomic status (SES), whether high or low. Coming from a higher SES, the upper middle-class child will have grown up possessing more advantages in the social structure, having been exposed to cultural influences that support the motives and skills necessary for higher attainment.[13] A child of similar capacity (as measured by IQ, for example, crude as it may be for equating capacities or

Table 1.2. *Departure from expected percentage[a] of males graduating from college among a sample of Wisconsin youths*

| | Intelligence levels | | | | |
Socioeconomic status	Low	Lower middle	Upper middle	High	Total
Low	001	036	050	092	034
Lower middle	010	034	077	158	065
Upper middle	020	045	112	214	100
High	048	107	177	293	193
Total	014	053	110	217	100
					(21.8%)
N	(1,070)	(1,100)	(1,083)	(1,133)	(4,386)

[a] Expected percentage represents the percentage of all males in the total sample who graduated from college: 21.8%. This expected value is divided into the obtained percentages for each condition or cell of SES × Intelligence level to index the departure from the expected value, and it is further multiplied by 100 to round out the values into whole numbers.
Source: Adapted from Sewell and Shah, 1967: 15.

potential), but with parents of lower SES, is more likely to be denied valuable activities and the culturally shared knowledge found in families of upper SES. Such limitations reduce the chances of graduating from college, regardless of capacity.

Of all males in this Wisconsin study, the percentage graduating from college was 21.8. We would expect more men with equal capacity but of higher SES to go beyond this norm, given their greater chances at learned skills, and the appropriate motives, related opportunities, and cultural supports. The converse should be true of males of equal capacity but lower SES. In fact, the relative advantage of a male of higher SES in completing college work shows up at every level of IQ (Table 1.2). Even at the highest IQ, the child from the lowest SES falls below parity (a score of 100), with a score of 092; the child at the highest level of both SES and capacity, on the other hand, exceeds parity by a score of 293, or 2.93 times that expected of the population as a whole. The ability of parents and other adults of higher SES to see that their children finish college is evident: their children's chances are consistently greater than those of equally talented children of lower SES. Sewell and Shah found that, among males, a high IQ contributed slightly more than a high SES to the likelihood of graduation from college. What is important is that the joint, contingent effect of both SES and IQ explained the obtained differences.

In general, educators recognize the importance of capacity or potential in college performance, as is evidenced in Sewell's analysis and will be shown in our data. On the other hand, the data demonstrate clearly that we lose educated talent when opportunities for exposure to necessary skills and motives are missing. To test this proposition, we attempted in our research to strengthen motives and skills, to expand opportunities, and to add education-supporting elements to the cultural mix being experienced by our respondents. We sought out youths who appeared, on the basis of tests and grades, to range from average to relatively high potential for college but looked for them in neighborhoods and schools unlikely to offer appropriate opportunities. Our experimental summer program and related follow-up activities were designed to increase participation of the pupils and their families in school programs and to support other educational, cultural, and social enterprises for them. At the same time, because social and cultural mobility can create psychological marginality, we attempted to devise pedagogical arrangements to stimulate adjustment to divergent social demands, with the aim of discovering whether bright students, exposed to a Middle Start program of greater opportunities and college-bound activities, along with related efforts to prepare them for upward mobility, would actually plan for and eventually attend college.[14] We wanted to find whether educational career lines were open to change at the age of thirteen — about the middle year of primary and secondary schooling — as a result of influences that could be duplicated fairly easily. There is strong evidence, from Sewell's research and elsewhere, that low SES strongly inhibits academic achievement, even in students of high intellectual capacity. Yet in the United States it is assumed that an extensive public education system can serve as a ladder accessible to all. We were concerned about the rungs missing from the ladders used by many students, and wondered if we could replace some of them.

This research, then, was applied to a program of intervention that tried to follow these directives: choose a population that is seriously disadvantaged educationally, intervene at a malleable stage, fit the intervention into as many aspects of a pupil's life as possible, continue it long enough to insure dependable effects, and gather the data necessary to guide shifts during the program and for systematic analysis and generalization afterward. The assessment, which ran parallel with the program, was longitudinal—experimental; it was applied to experimental and control populations that were paired randomly before the study rather than statistically *ex post facto.*

The experimental intervention entailed an intensive six-weeks' summer program of academic, artistic, and recreational activity, followed by a small-scale but continuous series of contacts through the succeeding five years. To make new opportunities visible, as well as available both to our students and to their families, we attempted not simply to describe norms and values supporting education, but to instill them in the several different sets of people important to our participants: teachers, college-age counselors, and our follow-up staff.

From our theoretical perspective it seemed unlikely that such structural and cultural changes would significantly affect achievement if individual interests and levels of skill were not raised simultaneously; therefore we chose the best teachers we could find for the summer program and made tutors readily available. We planned a mix of basic and self-selected courses that kept interest high, in the belief that many values, motives, and skills relevant to successful academic work had probably already been learned but might often have been inhibited. As we had neither the desire nor the need to remold our participants significantly, our task was to remove the barriers to the expression and development of tendencies already in the repertoire but blocked by lack of opportunity and of reward from peers and others. It was possible, we thought, that a "value-stretch" (Rodman, 1963) had led to the formation and acting-out of other tendencies, under conditions of limited opportunity and weak cultural support of academic work. Our aim was to create conditions under which intellectual and artistic interests could be readily expressed and strengthened.

We recognized that structural, cultural, and characterological factors were built into a tough system, sustained by the mutual reinforcement of factors. Hence temporary pressure on one factor (the motives and skills of individuals, for example) was unlikely to be effective. Only by attention to the whole field of forces could we hope to open up new alternatives.

Temporarily, it seems reasonable to suppose, we limited the options of students in the program, creating commitment by an intensive community experience (Kanter, 1972) that added the force of the group to individual forces. Options and commitments had also been limited, of course, by their earlier experiences. If freedom is the availability of alternatives, it was our hope that participants would be freer after the program, because more life chances would be realistically open to them.

Literature on educational intervention

Our concern for the cumulative influence of all the forces that act on children has drawn increasing encouragement from the literature on educational intervention. Never extensive, it emerged chiefly during the 1960s and is usefully reviewed by Gordon and Wilkerson (1966) in a compilation offering brief descriptions of the background and character of organized efforts in the United States that they were able to locate by a massive questionnaire mailing.

Gordon and Wilkerson revert to Binet's scientific interest in children whose intelligence, he thought, could be improved by training. They decry what happened afterward to the test developed by Binet to identify these children, and show how specialists shifted their attention from a systematic study of how to train minds, to quantitative methods of classifying intellectual status. This work, though often scientific, and sometimes useful in providing rigorous models for research, gave little attention to procedures for improving mental development. Gordon and Wilkerson think that recent efforts to improve ghetto children's intellectual performance would fare better if there had been more work over the past decades on exactly how strengths and weaknesses in the mind arise, and on how to stimulate or correct them.

They cite a second precursor to "crash" programs for the disadvantaged: the humanitarian-cum-scientific work of Maria Montessori with Italian slum children. She was a contemporary of Binet. Her work has been resurrected more often on behalf of advantaged middle-class children than of the disadvantaged. Nonetheless, Montessori developed highly specific methods of improving mental alertness in the very young. The doctrinaire rigidity of most Montessori disciples ever since the early twentieth century, however, did not encourage either flexible change or systematic analysis. Thus her techniques have not been as useful to current workers as they might have been.

From our point of view the most valuable contribution of Gordon and Wilkerson is their emphasis upon the "interactional" view of how children grow. This concept runs sharply counter to two others that command much attention today. Following the first, many programs in schools assume that a "backward" or "unproductive" child suffers a defect, and that improvement involves remedying that defect, once it has been carefully located. Any subnormal performance, then, merely needs specific attention to its locus. According to the second theory, any child who is below par in school is the victim, not of some internal personal deficit, but of a hostile or bare environment. The child must be given experiences to make up for the things his family and neighborhood do not provide, experiences that more favored children absorb from all about them as they grow to school age. The first view has been prevalent in the past; the second is fashionable today.

It is the thesis of our research that neither theory is sufficient. Both tend toward ethnocentric definitions of deficit, disregarding subcultural variations in language and valued behavior (see Labov, 1972). They also minimize interaction. The organism does not generally come first, with some built-in defect that hampers mental growth (although a very small proportion of children do, of course, have congenital handicaps). Nor is the environment able to work its effects directly, so that a rich and stimulating home automatically accounts for rapid development, a spare or frightening one for apathy. Instead, the field view assumes that both the organism and its environment work upon each other dynamically. Hunt, who has spoken powerfully for this idea (1961), shows that the effect of the environment on an individual depends upon whether prime time has arrived (Havighurst's "teachable moment"). He is most persuasive in noting that individuals, as they respond to their environment, may be sufficiently changed for them in turn to act upon and change it. Thus intelligence, far from being fixed (the constant-IQ assumption, dating from Binet), responds to its surroundings by changing its own traits. So the straightforward hereditarian or "traitist" and the simple environmentalist are both seeing only a part. In particular, they miss the effects of interaction.

Beyond these theoretical limitations are limitations upon experiment and action. The major interventions of the past decade have been on behalf of either preschool children or the much older high school dropouts; there is little comparable research on the middle school years. Agreeing that one-cause/one-effect patterns are too naive, Deutsch (1965) points out that the preschool and dropout programs both rest on unproved assumptions. Head Start (the federal government's application of some of Deutsch's own early research into linguistic development) assumes, as already noted, that "the earlier the better." Deutsch believes that this assumption may be justified; yet he notes that hard data are still wanting. "The earlier the better" is an especially vicious assumption if it fosters the rationalization that "after seven or eight years of age all is lost, because formation takes place in infancy." Efforts to salvage dropouts have usually been ineffective: they have come late and they have been relatively brief and incomplete. And because they have not been very successful, they, too, have given rise to an unfortunate claim that there is nothing to be done; the pattern is already set. Stages of growth not only have their own patterns (each can produce progress whether in due course or under remediation), but also they stretch out over connected experiences so that steady progress requires continual attention and long-term yet adaptable programs. Deutsch is wise when he inveighs constantly against short programs without enough follow-through.

Like Gordon and Wilkerson, Helen Astin (1972) prepared a comprehensive review of many of the intervention programs of the middle and late 1960s. Looking at the difficulties facing colleges when enrolling students who do not meet traditional entrance demands, Panos (1973), rather than insisting that the students assume all the burden of adaptation, argues that colleges must develop courses and services tailored to marginal students. The reward would be a large number of educated graduates to serve society. Alexander Astin (1971) and others have pointed out the serious inaccuracy of so-called aptitude tests in predicting the success of minority students in college.

The intervention described in our research accords with these various lines of advice voiced in the early sixties and in the years since then. It shuns a simplistic search for single causes of educational difficulties, preferring the requirement of field theory that activities be directed at the many facets of development. It assumes that junior high school pupils are still malleable. And it refuses to stop after a brief, if intensive, summer of stimulation, continuing instead to offer support over several critical adolescent years, albeit inadequately. Although research along these lines was rare in the early 1960s, by now many techniques have been tried, enlisting special teachers (reading, speech, etc.), special auxiliary professionals (counselors, physicians), and subprofessionals (student teachers and interns, lay specialists). Residential and day-school settings, ingenious teaching (teams, homogeneous groups, extended days), community cooperation — these alternatives and others have been tried in every part of the country. Important publicity has advertised pilot projects for inspiration and comparison, among them demonstration guidance systems in Harlem junior high schools, impressive efforts in New Mexico in behalf of children of Indian and Mexican backgrounds, Office of Economic Opportunity programs for children with latent or unrecognized talent, and the Ford Foundation's Great Cities Project. Probably the Rockefeller Panel Reports, *Prospect for America* (1961) which, as much as anything else, goaded interested persons to action by proclaiming the cost of wasting talent, have been of direct benefit mainly to high school juniors and seniors. And almost nobody has paid sufficient attention to systematic evaluation, either during or after a program.

Careful evaluation is the crux of the present book, this report, and in the area of evaluation, too, there was little material to draw on for almost every previous assessment had been made *ex post facto*. A number of important studies of this variety, although not primarily concerned with programs of educational intervention, raise significant methodological and substantive questions close to our interests. Several of them use statistical techniques, often quite sophisticated, to examine the characteristics of pupils whose circumstances have been changed, and to compare them with carefully chosen peers. The landmark assessment, the Coleman report (1966), was not so much a description of intervention as an analysis of the national situation after desegregation which, Coleman found, did raise the educational performance of minority students. He also concluded, however, that the home and neighborhood are such powerful forces that the quality of school as such has little impact. This generalization calls for careful specification of the circumstances under which it is true, partly true, or substantially false. The Coleman report also pointed to the unequal quality of schools across the country, the persistence of segregation, and the systematic differences between white and non-white achievement. But it was a cross-sectional study, albeit very well done.

The widely discussed book by Jencks and his associates, *Inequality: A Reassessment of the Effect of Family and Schooling in America* (1972), also utilizes cross-sectional aggregated data. It contains a lengthy discussion of background factors influencing academic performance. Although it does not deal directly with the influence of planned intervention on school performance under various conditions, its examination of the relationship between schooling and later income is closely related to our interests. In our judgment, Jencks' conclusion that there is little relationship between education and income is subject to serious misinterpretation, but to undertake a methodological critique here would take us too far afield. Insofar as he is saying that schools by themselves cannot be major instruments of social change or of income redistribution — that they are dependent variables to a substantial degree — we do not disagree. Or, if he is saying that efforts solely to increase equality of educational opportunity are not likely to go far toward the attainment of equality of educational achievement, the evidence supports him. But that is not the end of the story. His pessimistic outlook is strongly affected by the fact that he deals mainly with fairly modest efforts to change schools, or simply to change their racial composition — efforts that disregard the larger setting. Attention to the support of significant others, to the value placed on education by critical reference groups, to individual needs and motives, and to other variables is clearly necessary. When education is seen as part of the larger field of forces, its contribution — as we believe our study will show — can be significant. Jencks and his associates move too easily from macrosocial data to individual conclusions. Differentiating conditions among local situations and individuals must be specified.

Longitudinal research allows the effects of time to show up, and to show up in the same persons, year after year. In Wisconsin, Sewell has been following pupils into adulthood since the 1950s with sensitivity and skill. But he is quick to confess that such work, including his own, has to deal with what happens to take place.

Actually, the effects of schools and of other variables should be determined at least by longitudinal studies and at best by well-designed experiments in which students are assigned to schools at random or, if this is not possible — as it probably is not — there should be prior careful assessments of ability, family background, and other potentially confounding variables so that their effect can be controlled or appraised statistically. (Sewell, 1967: 478)

There is thus a hierarchy: cross-sectional studies are least powerful, longitudinal ones are a great improvement, but true experiments (with random assignment) are best. We know of no intervention into the lives of disadvantaged pupils where the experimental and control groups have evenhandedly come from the same pool, assigned at random. The comparisons that such an experiment permits are, of course, those most suited to generalization beyond the study itself. They are the best base for advice to inquirers who want to know what worked, what did not, and perhaps even why.

Following the work of Coleman, Sewell, and others, Chad Gordon

(1973) studied the sources of desire for education, in his case among ninth-graders. He used as independent and intervening variables: social class, race, self-esteem (with five aspects often consolidated into one "global" measure), family role structure (both parents at home, mother only, weak-male, and neither parent at home), parental aspiration, and verbal ability. As Gordon recognized, there are problems in conceptualizing and measuring most of these variables; because he used secondary data, he could not solve these problems, but he does make most of them explicit and interprets their possible effects skillfully. One or two issues require more examination than he gave them: Verbal ability scores on sixty questions were used as indexes of mental capacity. The author clearly recognized the cultural bias in the questions, but gave insufficient attention, in our judgment, to the implication of that fact. The "family role structure" variable has no time dimension. Thus a matriarchy may only recently have become one, the child having been influenced by a different pattern for most of his life. We have not yet learned how to handle such time-series problems.

Gordon found that "weak-male" families are not appreciably more common in working-class than in middle-class families, black or white. The weak-male type often appears as a negative referent, less likely to be associated with high verbal ability and high self-esteem in the children than the matriarchal family, although the patterns vary somewhat by class and race.

In a valuable combination of structural and personality variables, Gordon is able to explain 27 percent of the variance in desire for education among the black students and 45 percent among the white. Verbal ability, parental aspirations, and social class weigh most heavily in the outcome, with self-esteem and family role structure accounting for smaller, but still significant, proportions of the variance.

Questions of method are critical in evaluation of the review by Hunt and Hardt (1969) of Upward Bound programs, programs which share many qualities with our own educational experiment. Hunt and Hardt, reporting some general findings about the effect of Upward Bound on the attitudes, motivation, and academic achievement of black pupils, conclude that there are no discernible differences in grade point averages (GPAs) between chosen and unchosen students subsequent to the program. They insist on the importance of cumulative and innovative efforts to improve academic achievement and survival in future programming and funding.

Because major efforts to evaluate both types of federally supported programs of compensatory education (Upward Bound and Head Start) have relied on *ex post facto* matching procedures to generate control-group comparisons, a systematic discussion here may reinforce the lesson which the social science community must learn, namely, that program evaluation should not rely on *ex post facto* matching designs if they can be replaced by more powerful research designs, approximating true field experiments. Without such a standard we become embroiled in policy discussions that rest on findings with dubious foundations. When invalidating factors prevent clear attribution to the educational program itself, as is not uncommon in *ex post facto* studies (Campbell and Clayton, 1961), policy and funding questions are based on blind guesses about next steps.

Many examples of weak findings that influenced subsequent policy can be found in various reviews of the Head Start program.[15] Thus the Westinghouse-Ohio study implied that the program's effect had been negligible and even harmful. "In this context the Westinghouse-Ohio evaluation seemed to further demonstrate that public efforts to educate disadvantaged children were wasteful and futile. In February, President Nixon said that in view of the Report's findings, he would treat Head Start as an experimental rather than as an operational program" (Smith and Bissel, 1970). By this phrase President Nixon doubtless meant to downgrade the program and perhaps to indicate that it would be phased out. Strong public support, however, has kept Head Start alive. It is now becoming experimental in another sense: 5 percent of the children are involved in programs designed to add flexibility and to discover the most effective procedures (*New York Times,* June 8, 1975: 40). Full experiments in the technical sense have not yet been undertaken.

In the absence of such stringent tests, recipients of administrative largesse may fail to receive the maximum of direct and indirect benefits that the law intends. This is wasteful and futile. To assume that such consequences are intrinsic to educational intervention, however, is to run the risk of basing policy discussions and decisions on soft evidence (Ikeda, Yinger, and Laycock, 1970; Campbell, 1969; Lempert, 1966). Typical of *ex post facto* evaluation studies, Hunt and Hardt's research contains findings that are weak on at least two major points: the first is the reliance on an *ex post facto* matching procedure for control group data; the second is the absence of repeated nonreactive measurements of academic performance involving the use of several (multiple) indicators. Instead, they rely on cross-sectional comparisons of two cycles of students at different ages.

The exact procedure employed for *ex post facto* matched controls and 10-percent representative samples of cross-sectional data is described by Hunt and Hardt. In a survey of all pupils in target programs (21 out of 215 programs in 1966), the effect of the program upon attitude and motivation was measured by administering a battery of paper-and-pencil tests in the first week and the last week of the summer program and in the spring of the following academic year. Effect of the program upon the pupils' academic achievement was measured by collecting their GPAs from high school in June, before the summer program, and in February, after it. GPA results were also collected for control pupils not attending an Upward Bound program but whose preprogram GPAs were similar to those of the Upward Bound (UB) students.

GPA data were collected by locating a grade recorder in each of 189 high schools during the academic year 1966–67. Using the school records, each recorder first selected a non-UB pupil of the same sex and school grade with the same or nearly the same GPA, to match each UB pupil. Grade recorders were also urged to select a matched mate of the same ethnic or racial group and level of income; however, they were not always able to do so, with the result that the control group, while comparable in initial GPA, may not have been identical as to race or social class. Put another way, the 283 pupils in the control group may not all have met the criteria of being black and poor, but it is likely that most of them did so (Hunt and Hardt, 1969: 119, 127). Two critical questions are raised by this research.

(1) *Ex post facto* matching and regression artifacts: In the Hunt and Hardt research there is a strong likelihood that regression artifacts resulted from the post-treatment matching procedure. For one thing, the control subjects were less needy, which meant that the more needy were selected for the UB majority. If academic performance is positively correlated, even weakly, with the family's financial status, then the control group would tend to have better average grades, both pre- and post-test (Sewell and Shah, 1967 and 1968). Choosing control subjects whose family and academic profiles really match those of the UB pupils would lead to understating the potential and performance of the controls.

Campbell's comment on the weaknesses found in the Westinghouse-Ohio design applies to Hunt and Hardt's procedure:

[Post] Matching on several variables simultaneously has the same logic and bias (as is true of matching on a single variable). The use of multiple matching variables may reduce the regression artifact, but not remove it. It reduces it insofar as the multiple correlation of the several matching variables with the post-test is higher than the simple *r* of a single matching variable. Matching by means of qualitative dimensions or dichotomous variables has an equivalent bias. All such matching variables turn out to be imperfect indicators of the underlying variables we would like to match on. Parents' number of years of schooling have vastly different meanings from school to school, and within the same classrooms. Living in the same neighborhood or block means widely different things as far as the educational quality of the home is concerned . . . There is inevitably undermatching, in the sense that the population differences which one is trying to correct by matching are undercorrected by the matching process . . .

How can one tell which direction a matching bias will take? Only by having evidence on the nature of the population differences which matching had to overcome. Conceivably in reporting a matching process, the researcher might neglect to say what kind of cases he found hard to get matches for, and what kind of cases existed in surplus in the control population . . . [in the Head Start study] it was the most disadvantaged Head Starters that were hard to match and . . . the controls were selected from generally more able populations. (Campbell and Erlebacher, 1970: 9–10)

In the UB study, the regression artifacts operated in the selection of control subjects: the matches seemed never quite as disadvantaged as the pupils chosen for the UB program. If the latter also were chosen at the extreme of disadvantage, then regression effects of choosing the extremes of a population would also enter in (Campbell and Clayton, 1961).

The general effect of this treatment of control groups is to obscure any significant gains on the part of the UB participants — a result of the regression upward of the control group in the post-test of academic achievement.

(2) Measurement errors and biases in cross-sectional, single-measure studies: Lack of planning can result also in simplistic cross-sectional studies and in single indicators of an underlying variable. In the Hunt and Hardt study, academic performance is evaluated by GPAs in the case of younger and older pupils in the program, cross-sectional data being relied on for interpretation. It is not easy in the UB study to rule out peculiar historical and systematic maturational effects of going through high school. The finding that grade averages move in opposite directions among white and black participants also remains to be interpreted. The likelihood is that both historical and maturational factors interact with race. Without systematic replication of several cohorts

over a longer time, and lacking several other indicators of academic achievement — tests, graduation from high school, admission to college, and survival in the educational and occupational structures — we are left uncertain as to what Hunt and Hardt's findings tell us about the ways these variables affect each other.

To rule out biases and errors stemming from measurement and other features of design, Blalock suggests that multiple indicators be employed repeatedly:

> With a single measure of each variable, one can remain blissfully unaware of the possibility of measurement error, but in no sense will this make his inferences more valid. Though there is always the danger of becoming so hypersensitive to the possibility of measurement error that one becomes immobilized in the process, present practice seems to err in the opposite direction. Methodological studies . . . can help us see more clearly the nature of the step we must take if we are to become increasingly precise . . . I see no substitute for the use of multiple measures of our most important variables. (Blalock, 1970: 111)

Ex post facto studies typically neglect such considerations because of exigencies of time and funding.

In addition, for cyclical programs, repeating such measures (nonreactively, where possible) on a number of cohorts will uncover still better the invalidation caused by the newness of the program and its transient influences (see Cook, n.d.); essentially, it means obtaining reliable, multiple indicators of change (or nonchange) at several times. Thus errors due to temporary effects, to maturation related to systematic fluctuation in indicators, and to unique selection-treatment effects could be evaluated. Repetitive longitudinal measures are admirably suited to programs of compensatory (or almost any other) education.

2. Methods of the Middle Start program

The research reported in this book involves three related efforts to assess an educational program in a systematic way. First, we studied the effects of age by selecting pupils in the middle years of their schooling which, as will be explained below, we consider strategic in setting the life course. Although we did not directly introduce age as a variable, as our participants fell within a fairly narrow age range, our study does invite comparison with related research, most of which has dealt with very young children or with those in the last years of high school. Second, by randomly assigning prematched pupils we used a truly experimental field strategy that strengthened our ability to interpret the program's effects. Third, we followed our participants through several years (seven in the case of those in the earliest group), in order to measure long-run effects.

The origins of the Oberlin College Special Opportunity Program

In 1963, several members of the Oberlin College administration and faculty began to discuss institutional efforts to induce more talented youths from the minorities to aim at higher education and to recruit them for the college. Learning of possible Rockefeller Foundation support, the college created a faculty committee charged with two responsibilities: supervision of a college-level program of financial aid and supplemental educational services, and creation of a precollege program to prepare secondary-school youths for college. To support the precollege work, the foundation made awards to Oberlin, Princeton, and Dartmouth. While Dartmouth and Princeton — and most other institutions working at the precollege level — chose to help pupils in their last year or two of high school, Oberlin decided to bring a group of junior high pupils (mostly between seventh and eighth grades) to the campus for an intensive residential summer program. In the first summer, 1964, fifty-six pupils came to the campus from Cleveland, St. Louis, and three communities in the county near Oberlin (Lorain, Elyria, and Oberlin). The children from St. Louis and Cleveland were selected from schools located in neighborhoods which could be defined as "inner city." Two of the Cleveland schools from which the nominees came were predominantly black; in one the children were predominantly Southern-white migrant and Eastern-European ethnic. The St. Louis schools — in the Banneker District — were overwhelmingly black. Lorain contained a large Spanish-speaking population as well as both black and white migrant communities. Oberlin and Elyria were selected because of sizable concentrations of economically and educationally disadvantaged households of both races. Forty pupils had completed seventh grade; sixteen had completed the eighth. During the six summer programs that followed, only pupils who had just completed the seventh grade participated. The research deals with participants in the first three summer programs.[1]

Each summer program lasted six weeks. Although costs compelled us to shift to a day school during the last two summers, the three groups under study here were all in a residential program. The staff of teachers and counselors totaled about twenty during each of the summers, creating a rich staff—pupil ratio. The curriculum was deliberately broad, going well beyond the academic subjects, because we believed that a pupil, though eventually finishing secondary school, might have a limited general education. Therefore the staff sought to develop not only academic interests and skills, but others as well: aesthetics, physical activities, hobbies, personal and social sensitivity. In personal counseling, motivation and opportunity for higher education were examined intensively.

In 1966 the typical daily schedule was:

7:00:	breakfast
8:00—12:00:	classes
12:15—1:00:	lunch
1:00—2:00:	rest and guidance
2:00—3:20:	study, guidance, individual help
3:30—5:00:	swimming, bowling, modern dance
5:00—6:00:	free time
6:00—7:00:	dinner
7:00—8:30:	study

8:30—9:30:   individual tutoring, study, recreation
9:30—10:00:   snacks
10:00:   lights out

On weekends the schedule was modified to include field trips to plays and concerts, museums and factories, small-group work, individual tutoring, recreation, attendance at church, and free time.

Throughout the six weeks each pupil developed many close personal ties. These included a college student, who worked and lived with a small group of the children; a counselor, who held several individual and small-group sessions; teachers of academic and other subjects; and, of course, fellow pupils. Formal and informal records were kept. The staff met regularly to discuss pupils and the program and from time to time to make changes in response to opportunities and needs. It does not require statistical analysis to realize that the summer experience was intensive and sustained.

Postsummer follow-up

In order to strengthen the effects of the summer program, the sponsoring committee developed various follow-up activities, designed to maintain and enhance the pupil's interests and skills in academic competence, career planning, social and interpersonal competence, and extracurricular enrichment. There was no direct budget allocation for these purposes during the year after the summer program of 1964. In the next year, however, a director working one-fourth time was appointed. Part-time secretarial assistance was added to edit a newsletter, to plan some reunions during the summer, and to provide a book service to help students to develop personal libraries. The following year the director was on half time. Liaison persons, usually teachers in the schools involved, were appointed to assist in the development of school and parents' clubs. In the following year the summer director of the Special Opportunities Program was given a full-time appointment, which included responsibility for the follow-up described below. The differences in expenditure and in the range and quality of follow-up services may be responsible for different effects in the successive years: the 1964 summer participants received the least follow-up support at the beginning; increasing and earlier follow-up efforts were supplied to the 1965 pupils and even more to the 1966 pupils. Paradoxically, however, participants in the latter years received less attention in their last year of high school, a consequence of staff changes and depleted resources.

The postsummer activities, which became a regular part of our educational intervention, developed more slowly and less fully than, in retrospect, we wish had been true. Nevertheless, the follow-up program became an important part of the experimental stimulation. Beginning in the summer, we developed various arrangements to promote continuity. On the summer staff were teachers and counselors from the home schools who, in addition to serving as such, acted as liaisons between the summer program and the regular school, between Oberlin and home. Through them the program staff and the research staff each kept records, stimulated home contacts and school activities, and watched academic performance carefully.

We also made formal contacts with other important officials: administrators and guidance workers in the schools, research and supervisory staff "downtown," contacts necessary to insure continued activity on behalf of our pupils and regular access to their schools' records. In particular, as we reached out into the homes (for visits, interviews, and mutual planning for the pupils' futures), we became convinced that working through local school people already known and trusted would be better than sending in outsiders from the college. Summer staff recommendations were collated and sent to the schools to encourage local follow-up in course planning and counseling and so to make sure that each pupil took the courses likely to promote maximum attainment. Often this meant assignment to the college-bound track. It meant also being helped to succeed in required courses; hence counselors were apprised of any problems, and tutoring was arranged. At various times Oberlin representatives would reinforce the efforts of local people with reunions, talks, and individual sessions, in the belief that most school districts could sharpen their counseling and support of many bright but relatively unnoticed children from deprived backgrounds. We also encouraged parents' clubs, designed to inform the parents of participants in our summer program about advantageous school policies and opportunities, to tell them about financial aid accessible to disadvantaged pupils, and to keep the goal of further education alive.

Each group of pupils returned to Oberlin for a brief summer reunion during which academic and financial aspects of college attendance were discussed. They were encouraged to examine a wide range of colleges and to aim at one suited to their plans and aspirations. More frequently, participants from a given city and summer program met together to go on trips, to attend concerts or ball games, to see movies or hear talks, or to have a party. Some of those near Oberlin made their own way to campus occasionally to visit the college student who had been their summer leader, or to attend a game, concert, or play.

In our follow-up we did not try to dislodge the child from his original home—school—neighborhood setting. Rather, we encouraged the parents and the liaison staff in the schools to reinforce the pupil's best efforts to achieve in school — for one thing, by drawing upon available local resources and making them more visible to child, parent, and school staff. Thus the family remained intact within its setting, and our work did not isolate child or family from the realities of their environment.

To be sure, in the light of cumulative experience and policy reviews among follow-up staff, a few of our pupils were encouraged to move to a private, preparatory school. Some of these moves stemmed directly from efforts of the program staff; others came from the intense desire of the children and the families for improved schooling after the summer program. Neither alternative — that of returning them to settings which might limit their dreams and efforts nor that of placing them in new and possibly strange, novel, and even punishing environments — was comfortable to anyone. But educational, occupational, and community mobility requires children and families to confront changing and threatening social and cultural traditions; no educational program has yet found a way to eliminate the impact of changed social position (Ellis and Lane, 1967).

As our participants came closer to high school graduation, we tried to give them special attention, to make certain that they knew how to select a college and apply for admission, and that they actually did apply. Characteristics of college, financial aid, the necessary tests, application forms and recommendations were stressed. The staff responded to questions about specific problems; they supplied information about scholarships and encouraged pupils to apply for them, and made use of the newsletters, visits, and reunions to smooth the pupils' transition from high school to college.

Research questions raised by the follow-up program

Because we became more convinced, as the study continued, that follow-up activities were likely to increase the effect of the program significantly, we added more of them to the original research design. Limitations of time and money prevented us from adding as many contacts and stimuli as, in principle, we thought desirable. Nevertheless, the reunions, counseling, and newsletters became an integral part of the experimental variable. These additions raise three questions on which we reached judgments that we believe are soundly based even if not definitively answered and thoroughly confirmed.

First, how much are any observed results of the total set of experiences to be attributed to the summer program and how much to postprogram stimulation? Do the modifications make the original research design impossible to interpret? We believe not. Our judgment rests on the fact that the major parts of the research design — the summer programming and staffing and the selection procedures — remained constant.[2] Moreover, the summer program remained, as to the time involved, the number of change agents brought in, the resources expended, the depth of emotional impact, and other matters, the largest part of the stimulation. To separate that program definitely from the later activities would require three experimental groups, with matching control groups. We are confident, however, that it is the combination of influences which produced the observed results. To put it another way, we believe that the follow-up activities were important in the sense that a "booster shot" is important. Without it, the summer program would have been less effective. But of course a booster shot works only if there is something to reinforce. To some degree, our participants were entering a new cultural world, and each new experience was strange. Each activity, from the summer program on, helped prepare them in part for the next experience (shift to high school, application for admission to college, and the like), but never completely. Thus we were dealing with an integral stimulus, basically shaped by the summer experience, yet reinforced and modified thereafter.

Second, did the total stimulus vary in intensity from person to person, so that effects might be measured against different levels of involvement? Again, this would have been a useful variable, but to introduce it would have interfered with other elements of the plan: for example, with the desire to maximize the power of the stimulus over all participants, to keep the research design relatively simple, and to keep subgroups as large as possible, in order to increase the dependability of our measures. In fact, the range in intensity of stimulus was narrow. All pupils participated in the largest part of the program — the summer session — and most were influenced to some degree by follow-up activities. We have no measures that allow us to compare differences in intensity of the "same" experience — the extent to which pupils felt strongly caught up in the summer program, for example. The fact that only one dropped out of the summer session and that almost all attended the weekend reunion of the summer groups suggests that variance in intensity was not great. Doubtless, however, there are subtle differences that we have not detected; we can study only the fact of participation, not the depth.

Third, was labeling involved, so that any experimental results detected would be attributable more to reactions of teacher and counselor than to direct changes in performance by the students? This monograph is not the place to explore the large theoretical and experimental literature dealing with labeling. Deviation, mental illness, and educational—intellectual performance have frequently been examined in the light of it.[3]

The origins of labeling theory go back at least to G. H. Mead (the self is formed in interaction with and out of signals sent by significant others), W. I. Thomas (if men define situations as real, they are real in their consequences), and Robert Merton and R. M. MacIver (prophecies are often self-fulfilling). These and other theories have been shaped into the thesis that behavior is often the product of a label. This thesis has been developed in many different ways, however. A moderate version sees labeling as one cause in a sequence of interacting causes: pupils are labeled (let us say, for our interests, as bright or dull, educable or incompetent); they respond to the label; the response sometimes seems to confirm, and thus reinforces, the label which, being reissued, intensifies the response. Another version is more extreme: the power to label is the power to create an event. According to this interpretation, the deviant, the mentally ill, the intellectually incompetent are categorized not because they are significantly different from others, but because they occupy statuses or positions that make them vulnerable to definition by powerful others.

It is obviously important, not simply to our study, but to social science generally, to arrive at a correct statement of this issue. We cannot hope to do that here, but will state our perspective and indicate its import for our research. Although the extreme version of labeling theory brings forcibly to attention the power of labels in shaping human behavior, it overlooks many qualifiers that are necessary except in the limiting case: labelers often disagree with one another; most persons, after early childhood, have internalized tendencies that can at least partially deflect an undesired label; a large share of human interaction is shaped by the social structure and culture within which it is embedded. In short, the labeling process is one aspect of a complex system. That many authors tend to emphasize only negative labels limits the process unduly; full attention should be given, moreover, to self-labeling, which may show the influence of others' labels, but which also has its own sequences.

How do such ideas apply to our data? Do we have a "Pygmalion-in-the-classroom" situation, so that our participants seem to do well only because evaluators believe that they should be doing well? Or is their work improved only because, having been selected for special treatment, they continue to get more attention, more stimulation, more encouragement? We think there is almost no support for the first hypothesis and not much more for the second. It seems likely that the pupils in our program saw themselves in a somewhat different light after the summer's experience and that their families did so too, setting higher expectations and offering more encouragement. This "soft" version of self- and other-labeling seems to be part of the process. We think it quite unlikely, however, that labeling directly determined grades, achievement test scores, and persistence in school. Within a year after the summer program, the participants were scattered among many schools; few high school teachers knew about the program; and labels obviously could not determine outcomes on nationally scored achievement tests, except as they had influenced motivation and preparation leading up to the tests. In short, where labeling shades off into socialization, it is at work. Where it stands for a definition that then becomes a cause ("He must be bright, so we'll give him a high grade or admit him to college"), it seems to be minimally involved.

Selection procedures

Our research design called for pupils who had finished the seventh grade, two-thirds of whom were black and two-thirds male. We chose a majority of Blacks because in the early 1960s theirs appeared to be the most urgent need. We chose a majority of boys because efforts to help the entire disadvantaged community seemed more strategic when directed at prospective breadwinners. (This decision of 1964 may seem questionable today.) All of our pupils came from backgrounds that met specifications of economic hardship akin to those for Upward Bound programs.[4]

Our choice of pupils from the seventh and eighth grades reflected several considerations. Most of the programs with similar goals had concentrated their efforts on either younger children (e.g., Head Start) or on older adolescents in the last year or two of high school (e.g., Upward Bound). Thus, the group we selected had received relatively less attention. Although there is little doubt that a "head start" is preferable to a "middle start," programs devoted to educational stimulation of young children have had great difficulty in maintaining necessary follow-up activities — a problem we did not entirely escape — hence their effects fade. Programs that work with pupils in late adolescence, on the other hand, miss those who have already dropped out of school. In the case of those who have not dropped out, critical, career-determining decisions and learning may have taken place that set severe limits on possible new educational goals and performance. We believed that pupils in early adolescence would be more malleable than they would be later on, yet they were old enough to be away from home for a summer.

Another reason for our decision to dip down to the seventh grade stemmed from the recognition that early adolescence is a critical stage in the life cycle. Although the boundary between late childhood and early adolescence is probably best described as blurred and arbitrary, this period of progression through the system of age strata is generally marked by important transitions and role shifts. Most notably, entry into junior high school introduces a period during which "the sorting and selecting of individuals into alternative tracks becomes much more evident and increasingly less reversible" (Clausen, 1972: 472; Blos, 1971: 976; Kagan, 1971: 1005). An individual's choice among alternative tracks, as we noted before, is influenced by variable combinations of biological, structural, cultural, and personal factors. Such decisions, however, especially as they relate to academic aspirations and goals, can have lifelong consequences upon status attainment and mobility.

Early adolescence is also significant in that it is a time marked by greater independence and mobility, by a relative decline in the importance of the family as an agent of socialization, and by increasing interaction with and involvement in peer groups. Whether that peer group supports instrumental, future-oriented aspirations or, as Rainwater notes (1970: 286), "it validates a world view in which security and affluence will probably not come from conventional performance in schools and on the job but from learning how to hustle," may also have important consequences upon the remainder of the life course. This stage of adolescence, in other words, may be viewed as one in which dilemmas have to be resolved, uncertainties confronted, and models for the formation of identity selected (Ernest Campbell, 1969: 823–4; Gordon, 1971: 931–60; Kagan, 1971: 1007). From the perspective of the life cycle, therefore, our stimuli clearly came at a particularly important developmental juncture (Larson and Dittmann, 1975: 27–50).

The research design

Stated briefly, this is a study of the Special Opportunity Program's impact on the educational careers of the 195 students invited to participate in its first three years. Our final research design was a "patchy institutional cycle design" (Fisher's After-Only Design) with precision matching before random assignment. (The precision-matching method is described below.) As Campbell and Stanley note, a true experimental design (Fisher's After-Only Design) is more likely to control invalidity due to such factors as history, maturation, instrumentation, regression, and mortality, among internal sources of invalidity. Except for long-term effects of fatigue on researchers as observers (that is, as instrumentation), internally invalidating effects appear to have been well controlled. In general, we were able to obtain consent to the most powerful assignment procedures to form equivalent comparison groups.

We recognized that there would be "reactive leakage" between the chosen (Ex) and unchosen control group (C-1) children in the schools from which we asked for lists of eligible children, in view of the fact that those nominated were of similar levels of ability, shared some classes together, and thus may have known each other at school and in the neighborhood.[5] Leakage was reduced, however, by the fact that one year after the programs the participants in the larger cities, from which most of our students came, entered high school and were dispersed into different institutions, where they made up a very small percentage of enrollment. Probably some of the activities designed to help the experimental group, moreover, seeped into programs where both experimental and control children were enrolled, producing a conservative influence on our findings because, to an unmeasurable extent, such activities reduced the difference between the two, and thus lead to an underestimation of the effect of the experimental stimulus.[6]

Table 2.1 outlines the typical cycle of nomination, selection, participation, and evaluation of participation (or nonparticipation) in all three cycles of pupils under study. Within a given cycle, Cohort *A* included both the chosen (Ex) and unchosen (C-1) who were assigned from the school we invited to nominate children. Cohort *B* included the post-matched children from the postmatched schools (C-2) as well as a set of postmatched from the chosen schools (C-1-b). We sought the latter when we could not find adequate matches among the nominated pupils. We followed both cohorts through archival records of academic performance, by interviews, and by questionnaires mailed to the heads of the childrens' households. The archival checks are less reactive; the other checks may be quite reactive.

The method of prematching before random assignment, although it greatly enhanced internal validity, limited our ability to generalize to the total nominated and eligible list. Matches could not be found for all who were nominated. Our main effort, therefore, was to establish the size and direction of differences within the study itself. Talent searches that are better able to match the whole range of students can deal more effectively with questions of external validity and can generalize more broadly (Campbell and Erlebacher, 1970: 192–6).

The quality of the matching

The best plans for selection of experimental and control subjects by use of prematching on several variables are limited by various field conditions. Our most common difficulty was a school nomination list that was too short or too heterogeneous to permit good matches. To indicate the range of such problems, we prepared a scale of ability to control the matching process, ranging from matches in which the investigators had full control to those which involved postmatching and its inherent weaknesses, in particular, the absence of random assignment. Although most of our matches fall in categories 1 and 2, as shown in Table 2.2, others are scattered throughout the range.

In our interpretation we take account of the quality of the matches resulting from these various procedures, and also study variation in the quality itself as a variable, to determine whether it influenced the outcomes.

Table 2.1. *A patchy institutional cycle design (modified design #15)*

Experimental and control groups within cycle (repeat for 3 cycles)	Experimental treatment (multiple treatments extended over five years)	Measurement	
		Nonreactive measures	Reactive measures
Cohort A (pupils nominated, prematched[a] and assigned from chosen school)		Design #6: After-Only Fisher Design expanded into Design #15	
Ex group Selected randomly to participate	Received treatment		
C-1 group Selected randomly to serve as controls	Did not receive treatment	Archival measures from school records	Interviews and mailed questionnaires
Cohort B (pupils postmatched with Group 1 students)		Design #10: Nonreactive, postmatched, nonequivalent control group expanded into Design #15	
C-1-b group Postmatched within chosen school			
C-2 group Postmatched from unchosen school			

[a]The first cycle of pupils in 1964 was assigned by simple random assignment rather than by prematching before assignment. Postmatching of nonequivalent matches within the nominated, eligible group was also done.

Table 2.2. *Types of matching*

	N
1. Paired by research team from original nominated list; random choice from pairs, one as experimental pupil, one as C-1 pupil.	55
2. Experimental group chosen by team randomly from entire nominated list; C-1 pupil matched by team later from original nominated list.	43
3. Experimental student chosen by team, but not randomly from entire list; C-1 pupil matched by team later from original nominated list.	34
4. Experimental group chosen by school authorities; C-1 pupil matched by team later from original nominated list.	9
5. Experimental pupil chosen by team, but not randomly from entire list; no satisfactory match from original nominated list; C-1 pupil matched by team later from further suggestions or nominations from school authorities.	20
6. Experimental pupil chosen by team, but not randomly from entire nominated list; no satisfactory match from original nominated list; C-1 pupil matched by team later from school records of pupils not originally or later nominated or suggested by school authorities.	33
7. Other	1
Total	195

The role of matching in sociological experiments

To impute causal effects to experimental treatments, one seeks to establish equivalence in initial characteristics between experimental and control groups by any of several possible methods. The most general procedure, once thought to produce precisely equivalent groups, is pretesting. This is no longer seen as adequate, however, because pretesting, by sensitizing respondents to the experiment, may modify its influence. Unless one wants to measure the effects of pretesting itself, a better procedure is to assign experimental and control groups randomly from a given population pool — the Fisher After-Only design — the preferred method if the pool is large. When the number of eligible participants is small, however, and the population heterogeneous, random assignment without initial controls on the probable heterogeneity can lead to the conclusion of no difference between control and experimental subjects, when in fact they are different, or to an equally spurious conclusion of difference. Such misleading results are due to interaction between the

experimental stimulus and initial, uncontrolled differences among respondents (for fuller discussion of these issues see Yinger, Ikeda, and
Laycock, 1967).

There are various ways to avoid or reduce these difficulties. If there
are fairly clear-cut strata in the population, division into homogeneous
subsets is valuable. When few persons are available for assignment into
control and experimental groups, however, stratification is not feasible.
The alternative is to match pairs of subjects before random assignment.
Although this matching reduces the extent to which findings can be
generalized to a wider population (because of the loss of nonmatchable
cases) it can help to insure initial equivalence. A further step, the use of
matching in conjunction with random assignment to experimental and
control groups, increases the precision of interpretation. As Campbell
and Stanley note:

matching can be recognized as a useful adjunct to randomization but not as a substitute for it; in terms of scores on the pretest or on related variables, the total population available for experimental purposes can be organized into carefully matched
pairs of subjects; members of these pairs can then be assigned *at random* to the
experimental or to the control conditions. Such matching plus subsequent randomization usually produces an experimental design with greater precision than would
randomization alone. (1963: 219)

After use of these procedures to increase precision, an analytic procedure must be chosen that will take account of the multiple effects of
the matched variables as they interact with the experimental treatment.

These issues were in our minds as we began the research. To discover
whether our intervention had produced the desired effects, we needed
measures, over several years, of the educational performance not only of
the children in the program but also of those in the control groups. Most
of the 390 who made up the core of the study had just finished the
seventh grade at the time we began our observations. (The number of
matched pairs in any particular analysis ranges downward from 195,
depending upon the availability of certain kinds of information.) The
children came from five cities and fourteen schools. Before selecting the
participants, we asked the several school systems to nominate at least
twice as many as they were entitled to send. We paired the children on
the basis of several criteria, using information on a data form with
which we had furnished the schools and then we randomly assigned one
from each pair to the experimental group and one to the control group.

Several departures from ideal matching were, however, inevitable.
Sometimes information about father's occupation, or a full record of

school grades was missing. In a few instances during the first year school personnel, either because of misunderstanding or a powerful (and understandable) urge to reward their "best" children, sent us a list of appointed children and the "alternatives" — a procedure that restricted randomization. Most important, the lists from which we drew the selections were seldom more than twice as large as the number to be selected, limiting the range of variables we could take into account. From the point of view of *external* validity, to be sure, there is some advantage in having to match nearly 100 percent of the individuals. There can be very little exclusion of those who are difficult to match — an exclusion that can produce a systematic bias (Freedman, 1950: 485–7) — but there is also the disadvantage that the match will necessarily be rougher. The question is, how much rougher, and how is the imprecision to be measured? (For a discussion of external and internal validity, see Campbell and Stanley, 1963.)

Despite these problems, common in field research, we undertook to approximate precise matching as closely as we could. Ideally, we would have matched, for example, a thirteen-year-old black boy from a given school in St. Louis with another thirteen-year-old black boy from the same school, both of them with C+ academic averages, IQs of 108, who had similar results on other tests, who each had two older brothers and three younger sisters, fathers who were semiskilled workers living in the home, mothers who were housewives, each of whom had finished the ninth grade, and so on.

In practice, we matched on eight variables: ethnicity, sex, class in school, city, school district (and, except for St. Louis, school within the district), father's place in the household, academic and intelligence measures; and then we randomized. This is the point at which matching usually stops. Research workers and their reviewers then tend to take one of two positions: either they stress the number and seriousness of the compromises from the ideal model, note the need for caution in interpreting the data, and call for further research; or they note the care used in matching as closely as possible, emphasize the beneficent statistical effects of randomization, and hope for the best.

Measuring the quality of the matching

Not being comfortable with either alternative, we designed two indexes of matching quality to tell how closely we actually matched pairs of individuals.

There are several arbitrary qualities in such indexes of congruence among matched persons or units. Which variables should be employed in the match (to control unwanted influences), and which should be allowed to vary? If an index is a *scale* of initial equivalence or nonequivalence, how should each variable be weighted? How large should the quantified categories be to indicate similarity or difference? How should effects of interaction be treated (Blalock, 1965)? This last is a particularly troublesome question, because empirical support and underlying theory about choices of important effects of interaction are not well developed. It seems plausible, for example, that the variable "mother works outside the home"/"does not work outside the home" interacts with another variable: "father present"/"father absent." It may also be modified by presence or absence of older siblings, by ethnicity, and by other variables.

An "ideal" match. We attempted in various ways to take such interaction into account and to remember the arbitrary aspects of our indexes. With these cautions in mind, we first selected sixteen variables for what we called an ideal index; we assigned them various weights, and determined how they would be combined into one significant figure. Table 2.3 shows procedures by which this Index of Congruence was formed.

The result of these procedures was a scale whose scores ranged from 0 to 64. These are arbitrary numbers, of course, which acquire meaning only when used comparatively. A score of 0 indicates a "perfect" match within the definitions used; 64 indicates maximum possible measured difference; any score near the high end of the range indicates a serious flaw in matching. To illustrate: a score of 10 may encompass the following departures from a perfect match (with number in parentheses indicating extent of departure from a good match): a seven-months' difference in age (1), father in one home, another adult male (grandfather) in the other (2), one adult male with four years of schooling, the other with nine (2), one mother with eight years of schooling, the other with ten (1), one of the pair without sisters and with two fewer siblings (2), one stanine difference in IQ (1), and a .70 difference in average grades (1). At first we used negative numbers for each departure from a good match to emphasize to ourselves the need for caution in interpretation. Positive numbers, however, are probably simpler to use. In any case, the higher the score, the poorer the match.

A directional match. The procedures described so far are based on a strict definition of a good match. Low scores can be obtained by these

Table 2.3. *Index of Congruence*

		Range of possible difference between members of matched pairs in points
1. Ethnicity or race		0 to 4
White—White Black—Black "Spanish"—"Spanish" etc.	= 0	
"Spanish"—White Black—"Spanish" Other non-White—White Other non-White—Black	= 2	
Black—White	= 4	
2. Age		0 to 2
Under 6 months difference	= 0	
6 months to 11 months difference	= 1	
Over 12 months difference	= 2	
3. Sex[a]		0 to 3
Same	= 0	
Different	= 3	
4. City of residence[a]		0 to 2
Same	= 0	
Different	= 2	
5. School attended		0 to 1
Same	= 0	
Different	= 1	
6. Status of father in home[b]		0 to 5
(Points are calculated by finding the numerical difference between members of the pair, using the following scale. Use highest number applicable.)		
0. Father unknown; no other adult male in home		
1. Father not in home, but alive; no other adult male in home		

Table 2.3 (*cont.*)

	Range of possible difference between members of matched pairs in points
2. Father dead; no other adult male in home	
3. Other adult male in home	
4. Stepfather in home	
5. Father in home	
7. *Father's occupation (or that of other adult male)*	0 to 4
(Calculate as above)	
0. No adult male in home	
1. Unskilled	
2. Semiskilled	
3. Skilled	
4. White-collar or semi-professional	
8. *Education of father (or that of other adult male)*	0 to 4
(Calculate as in item 6)	
0. No adult male in home	
1. Father or other adult male with less than 5 years of education	
2. 5 to 8 years of education	
3. 9 to 11 years of education	
4. High school graduate or higher	
9. *Status of mother in home*	0 to 4
(Calculate as in item 6)	
0. Mother not in home, but alive	
1. Mother dead; no other adult female in home	
2. Other adult female in home	
3. Stepmother in home	
4. Mother in home	
10. *Employment status of mother (or of other adult female) during most of the preceding year*	0 to 3
(Calculate as in item 6)	

Table 2.3 (*cont.*)

	Range of possible difference between members of matched pairs in points
0. No adult female in home 1. Housewife 2. Part-time work 3. Full-time work	
11. *Occupation of mother (or of other adult female)* (Calculate as in item 6) 0. No adult female in home 1. Housewife, unskilled, or semi-skilled 2. Skilled 3. White-collar or semi-professional	0 to 3
12. *Education of mother (or of other adult female)* (Calculate as in item 6) 0. No adult female in home 1. Mother or other adult female with less than 5 years of education 2. 5 to 8 years of education 3. 9 to 11 years of education 4. High school graduate or higher	0 to 4
13. *Sibling patterns*	0 to 6

13. *Sibling patterns*

(Several of these statements may apply to a pair. They are additive up to 6 points.)

a. Only child in both cases   = 0
   One an only child, the
   other not   = 1
b. Both eldest children   = 0
   One the eldest, the other not   = 1
c. Both have or neither has
   siblings of the same sex   = 0
   One has siblings of same sex,
   the other does not   = 1

Table 2.3 (*cont.*)

		Range of possible difference between members of matched pairs in points
d. Both have or neither has siblings of opposite sex	= 0	
One has siblings of opposite sex, the other does not	= 1	
e. Difference of one or no difference in number of siblings	= 0	
Difference of 2 or 3 in number of siblings	= 1	
Difference of 4 or more in number of siblings	= 2	
14. *Intelligence quotients*		0 to 8
(Different tests and dates having been equated, where necessary by translation into stanines)[c]		
Same stanine	= 0	
Different stanine	₁ = 1 to 8	
15. *Achievement tests*		0 to 8
(Different tests and dates having been equated, where necessary by translation into stanines)		
Same stanine	= 0	
Different stanine	= 1 to 8	
16. *Grades (average of 7th-grade scores in "solid subjects." 4 = A; 3 = B; 2 = C; 1 = D)*		0 to 3
0− .49 difference	= 0	
.50− .99 difference	= 1	
1.00−1.49 difference	= 2	
1.50 and more difference	= 3	

[a] In practice, there were no mismatches on these variables and only one on the first variable.

[b] The effect of calculations based on variables 6−8 is to produce an "advantage score" relative to models of adult males. The sharpest contrast possible would be between a child whose father is unknown and one who lives with his real

methods only if the original pool from which the experimental and control groups were selected was large (making it more likely that one can find matched combinations) and if the experimental and control groups were large, to give free play to randomization. These procedures may, however, be too stringent for some purposes. The good match they demand does not include — as theory may — the cancelling-out effects of two mismatched variables. If we assign direction to the influence of some variables, we may be justified in saying that a person with a score of -1 on variable A and $+1$ on variable B is well matched with a person whose scores on the same variables are the reverse. In the model described above, such a pair would have two negative scores, but a directional model of matching would record the score as zero.

On the basis of previous research and theoretical considerations, therefore, we also designed a Directional Index. At first, we considered five predictors of academic success: (1) a composite score on father's status (derived from information on three variables: level of education, occupation, and presence or absence from home); (2) a similar composite score on mother's status, based on four variables; (3) an intelligence test score; (4) various achievement test scores; and (5) grade-point averages. Thus we were dealing with ten variables consolidated into five clusters. We also factored these five predictors (involving ten measures) using the data from our respondents, and four factors emerged, the third and fourth items above collapsing into a single factor. The close similarity of the predictor variables in the original Directional Index to the results of the factor analysis allowed us to use the more stringent measures without changing our original design. Since subsequent analyses were based on both the original Directional Matching Index and the results of the factor analysis, the construction of each measure of matching is described below in greater detail.

The ten variables used in both the original Directional Index and those that emerged from the factor analysis were:

Table 2.3. (*cont.*)

father, who is a white-collar worker or semiprofessional with at least a high school education.

[c] Among various methods of making comparisons among persons who have taken different tests, use of their stanine scores seems most generally valuable. Most of our pairs took the same test during the same year, so intertest comparisons are uncommon. Although there is the theoretical possibility of an 8-point difference (if one of a pair fell in stanine 1, the other in stanine 9), the empirical difference seldom exceeds 3.

1. father in the home
2. father's occupation
3. father's education
4. mother in the home
5. mother's employment status
6. mother's occupation
7. mother's education
8. preprogram IQ scores
9. preprogram achievement test scores
10. grade-point average in seventh grade

To obtain the original Directional Matching Index we combined scores on the following items (variable numbers refer to Table 2.3):

1. *Composite score on father's status*

A. Educational comparison (see variable 8)

$+2$ = Ex 3 or 4 higher
$+1$ = Ex 1 or 2 higher
0 = educ. equivalence
-1 = C 1 or 2 higher
-2 = C 3 or 4 higher

B. Occupational comparison (see variable 7)

$+2$ = Ex 3 or 4 higher
$+1$ = Ex 1 or 2 higher
0 = Occ. equivalence
-1 = C 1 or 2 higher
-2 = C 3 or 4 higher

C. Status in home (see variable 6)

$+2$ = Ex 3 or more
higher
$+1$ = Ex 1 or 2 higher
0 = equivalence
-1 = C 1 or 2 higher
-2 = C 3 or more higher

2. *Composite score on mother's status*

A. Educational comparison

(as above)

B. Occupational comparison

I. Status
(see variable 10)
$+1$ = Ex 2 or 3,
C 0 or 1
0 = Both 2 or 3,
or 0 or 1
-1 = C 2 or 3,
Ex 0 or 1

II. Skill
(see variable 11)
$+1$ = Ex 2 or 3,
C 0 or 1
0 = Both 2 or 3,
or 0 or 1
-1 = C 2 or 3,
Ex 0 or 1

C. Status in home

(as above)

These operations yield possible scores ranging from $+6$ to -6 on variables 1 and 2.
Reduce each to a 4-point contrast in the following way:

$$\left.\begin{array}{l} +6 \\ +5 \end{array}\right\} = +2$$

$$\begin{array}{l} +4 \\ +3 = +1 \\ +2 \end{array}$$

$$
\begin{array}{l}
+1 \\
0 \;=\; 0 \\
-1 \\
\hline
-2 \\
{} \;=\; -1 \\
-3 \\
\hline
-4 \\
-5 \;=\; -2 \\
-6
\end{array}
$$

3. *Intelligence tests (sixth or seventh grade)*

+2 = Ex 2 or more stanines ahead
+1 = Ex 1 stanine ahead
 0 = same stanine
−1 = C 1 stanine ahead
−2 = C 2 or more stanines ahead

4. *Achievement tests (sixth or seventh grade)*

(as above, in 3)

5. *Grades in seventh grade "solid" subjects (English, science, mathematics, social studies), average on 0–4 point scale*

+2 = Ex 1.00 or more ahead
+1 = Ex .50–.99 ahead
 0 = neither more than .49 ahead
−1 = C .50–.99 ahead
−2 = C 1.00 or more ahead

These operations yield possible Directional Matching Index scores ranging from +10 to −10. As only two of the 195 pairs, however, were outside a +5 to −5 range, we consolidated it into a +5 to −5 scale.

A factor analytic approach to directional matching. The factor analysis that was performed on the set of ten preprogram status variables used an iterative kind of principal component analysis in order to improve the estimates of the communalities with each successive iteration. The initial estimates of the communalities were based on the squared multiple correlations of the given variable with all other variables in the analysis.[7] A set of factors was then extracted based on this initial estimate; subsequent estimates were based on the percentage of variance explained by the extracted factors. The iterative procedure continued until the difference between consecutive iterations for all communality estimates was less than .001. The final set of extracted factors was rotated to maxi-

Table 2.4. *Factor loadings after oblique rotation*

Variable	Loading on factor 1	Loading on factor 2	Loading on factor 3	Loading on factor 4
Father in home	.65	.20	−.01	.01
Father's occupation	.58	−.16	.03	−.00
Father's education	.88	−.00	.04	.01
Mother in home	.05	−.23	.12	.04
Mother's employment status	−.12	−.61	.01	.04
Mother's occupation	.01	−.81	−.08	−.05
Mother's education	.05	−.29	−.09	−.23
IQ test	.01	.06	−.83	.10
Achievement test	.02	−.14	−.36	.54
Seventh grade GPA	.00	.02	.00	.46

mize the variance explained by the first, then the second, the third, and the fourth factor. Given the interrelations of the variables analyzed, orthogonality of factors was not assumed and oblique rotation was performed instead. The choice of these particular four factors was based on the magnitude of the eigenvalue associated with each factor (in this case, an eigenvalue greater than 1.00).[8]

Table 2.4 shows the factor loadings of the ten variables for each of the four factors. Loadings we used to interpret the factors are in italic. Each of the factors in Table 2.4 appears to have a straightforward meaning. Factor 1 is the status of the father; Factor 2 is the status of the mother; Factor 3 is the educational potential of the child; and Factor 4 is the child's prior educational achievement. We used these four factor scores in the main analysis to represent our measurement of preprogram advantages of the experimental over control subjects.

Table 2.5 indicates the variance explained by each of the four factors extracted from the ten variables. Although we rotated obliquely, the actual intercorrelation among the factors is fairly close to orthogonal (Table 2.6). Only the correlations between Factors 2 and 4 and between Factors 3 and 4 are large enough to assume obliqueness.

The analysis for each child, then, yielded four factor scores: father's status, mother's status, tested potential, and educational achievement. A revised Directional Matching Index was based on the differences between the experimental and control pair on these four scores. We defined it as an index of similarity in preprogram educational and status profiles between an experimental and control child. We obtained it by

Table 2.5. *Percentage of total variance explained by the factors*

Factor	% of total variance
1 (Father's status)	20.2
2 (Mother's status)	18.4
3 (Test potential)	15.2
4 (Educational achievement)	10.1
Total	64.0

Table 2.6. *Factor correlations*

	Factor 2	Factor 3	Factor 4
Factor 1	−.07	.08	−.07
Factor 2		−.06	.16
Factor 3			−.21

measuring the difference between the experimental and the control partner on each factor score, which we then recoded as shown in Figure 2.1. The plus sign indicates an advantage to the experimental child, while the minus sign indicates an advantage to the control child. The Matching Index, which has a theoretical range of −16 to +16, is the sum of these recoded differences for the four summary measures.

These factor scores reduce the effect of unstable estimates of underlying variables, which could arise if we had relied on a single item or score (Brewer, Campbell, and Crano, 1970). In complex partialling operations, whether the procedure be partial correlation or multiple classification analysis, such instability in single items can result in serious under- and overestimation of effects.

Use of the Matching Indexes. Before concluding that the experimental variable has produced any observed results, we shall trace their relation-

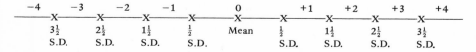

Figure 2.1. Range of advantage–disadvantage among matched pairs.

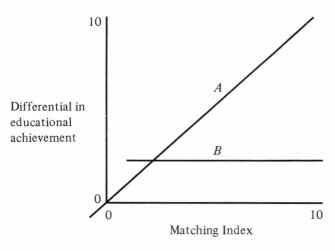

Figure 2.2. Illustrative correlations between Matching Index scores and differential achievement scores, among matched pairs

ship to the matching indexes. In statistical terms, a high coefficient of correlation between the matching index scores (with high scores indicating a poor match) and a score indicating differentials in educational achievement between experimental and control pairs will cast doubt on the interpretation that the experimental stimulus produced the observed differences in educational outcomes. Conversely, a low correlation between the matching indexes and measures of change will support our hypothesis. Thus line *A*, (Figure 2.2), would not support the proposition that differences in matched pairs were produced by the program, but line *B* would. (This statement assumes a linear relationship. If, in fact, the relationship is curvilinear, in the form of a U-shaped curve, for example, more complex interpretations would be required.) The actual relationship is close to line *B* (see Chapter 4); the coefficients of correlation (.14, using the original data and .03, using the factor scores) are not significant.

Measures of initial and long-term impact

We sought to measure the impact of our program with instruments that had some chance of applying uniformly to both chosen and unchosen nominees. Most of the measures were nonobtrusive and nonreactive. The following instruments were developed and employed.

The pupil data form

We used this form for both chosen and unchosen children, to obtain the total list of *nominated* students from the schools. We prematched before random assignment from these forms, selection being determined by the criteria reported above.

The pupil's permanent record form

After a careful review of the permanent record forms of pupils in the five school districts and any variant forms from other schools to which they transferred, we developed a standard form for recording selected academic information, covering pre- and postprogram measures of the following variables:

1. Grades over the study period, usually semester by semester, on a 4-point scale.
2. Test scores on achievement and intelligence, usually converted to stanine scores.
3. Academic track, where applicable, and related information on curriculum, especially whether college-preparatory or not.

We were aware that grades, tests, and tracking are to some degree culturally biased; however, some of the difficulties thus introduced may be avoided by use of a matching design, because any distortion presumably bears equally on experimental and control subjects, equated as to race and class. Certain advantages of such nonreactive measures to some degree offset the disadvantages. For one thing, the research findings are less affected by the research process. Moreover, even culturally biased measures may predict future performance in college or other settings where the culture reflected in the measures is dominant. For these reasons we employed school grades, achievement and intelligence test scores, and school track in comparing our participants with their control partners.[9]

Nevertheless, we need to be alert to the problems associated with their use in research. We can illustrate the problems posed by the pervasiveness of culture by discussing one in particular that affects even matching studies. It is based on a difficulty found throughout the country: the variation in the awarding of grades to pupils who are assigned to different academic tracks. In some schools — probably the majority, although there is no way to be sure — teachers give superior grades to all pupils in the top track; in others, they use the full range of grades in each class, regardless of track. The first policy deals with a larger population (the entire sophomore class, for example), and assigns marks based on everybody's achievement. Pupils in the top track usually achieve the most, so they all earn relatively high grades. The second policy takes each classroom separately and gives the highest grades only to the best performers in the room. Pupils, of course, find out which policy is used: after all, they are curious to know whether everyone in a top-track class automatically gets high grades.

Unfortunately, it is not easy to tell on what basis a given teacher gives out grades. Even where a district-wide policy is supposed to be followed, individual teachers may not follow it rigorously. Where there is no broad policy, a principal may try to impose one in a particular school, with different degrees of success from class to class; or each teacher may decide how to grade on whatever basis seems to make sense. The trouble is that archival records give no clues to grading policy.

This confusion entered our research because most of our pupils were tracked in high school. Half the experimental pupils (97 of 195) spent more than half their time in top-track classes, in contrast to only one-third (60 of 195) of the controls. Therefore we interpreted their grades cautiously. We could not know whether an A represented the best work in a top-track class or only typical work, nor could we know what an A meant in other tracks.

When we move from teachers' grading practices to the effect that tracking has on their pupils, the problem is compounded. A classic defense of segregating the brightest pupils is that they then come together in a group that stimulates them all to a high degree. When superstimulation occurs, pupils usually work much harder and, as their achievement rises, higher grades should result. On the other hand, giving everybody the same high grades may weaken attitude and depress productivity, although we know of no evidence of this.

We therefore could not say with assurance what was the effect of tracking on achievement, if we concentrated on grades for evidence. We had to refer to other measures as well, notably scores on achievement tests, which provide something of an outside check on teachers' grades, because they are based on nationwide norms rather than local practices. We were able to get comparable information on grades, tests, and quality of schooling for 441 out of 484 pupils (91 percent), despite the dif-

Table 2.7. *Archival information*

	1964			1965			1966			Total		
	Data	n	%	Data	n	%	Data	n	%	Data	n	%
Ex	49	56	88	66	70	94	63	69	91	178	195	91
C-1	52	56	93	65	70	93	62	69	90	179	195	92
C-2	23	24	96	26	33	79	35	37	95	84	94	89

ficulties in dealing with five school boards and administrations. The rate of return is shown in Table 2.7.

Parents' interview schedule

To deal consistently with the individual most likely to influence the education of the children, we sought the mother or other appropriate woman of the house. The following topics were central to the interview:

1. A description of family resources and conditions affecting ability to provide financial support and to guide the child toward academic achievement.
2. The adult's educational and occupational aspirations for the child.
3. The adult's access to and confidence in reference persons and groups who could guide the child to educational and occupational achievement.
4. Motivation and attitude in the home toward achievement, especially optimism or pessimism about educational and occupational mobility.
5. Adult opinion about the impact of the Special Opportunity Program.
6. Demographic data on the family or household.

These interviews took place during the twenty-six months from June 1968 through July 1970, four years after the summer program. Most of the interviewers were of the same race as the respondents. We held interview training sessions in each of the five cities (Table 2.8).

The mailed questionnaire

Our most recent information came from a questionnaire mailed to both participant and nonparticipant households. In four successive mailings

Table 2.8. *Interviews*

	1964			1965			1966			Total		
	Completed	n	%	Completed	n	%	Completed	n	%	Completed	n	%
Ex	49	56	88	64	70	91	62	69	90	175	195	90
C-1	37	56	66	50	70	71	52	69	75	139	195	71
C-2	18	24	75	30	33	91	33	37	89	81	94	86
	Refused[a]			Refused			Refused			Refused		
Ex	3			0			1			4		2
C-1	1			7			3			11		6
C-2	4			2			2			8		9
	No contact[b]			No contact			No contact			No contact		
Ex	4			6			6			16		8
C-1	18			13			14			45		23
C-2	2			1			2			5		5

[a] Of the refusals, 15 were White, 8 were Black, none was American of Spanish-speaking descent.
[b] Moved out of area, or were not located through any public source.

Table 2.9. *Questionnaire and counselor returns*

	1964		1965		1966		Total	
	n	%	*n*	%	*n*	%	*n*	%
Ex	(56)		(70)		(69)		(195)	
Questionnaire	45	80	59	84	56	81	160	82
Counselors and								
other sources	11	20	11	16	11	16	33	17
No info	0		0		2	3	2	1
C-1	(56)		(70)		(69)		(195)	
Questionnaire	33	59	48	69	44	64	125	64
Counselors and								
other sources	22	39	18	26	20	29	60	31
No info	1	2	4	6	5	7	10	5
C-2	(24)		(33)		(37)		(94)	
Questionnaire	17	71	27	82	23	62	67	71
Counselors and								
other sources	6	25	5	15	13	35	24	26
No info	1	4	1	3	1	3	3	3

we had replies from 352 households, to which we added information from school counselors, who had obtained parallel data in their annual interviews with students about academic and occupational planning (Table 2.9).

Thus we had data from postprogram questionnaires or counselors' reports from 97 percent of the subjects of the study, a rather remarkable rate of return, given the backgrounds of the households. It probably matches the rate in Sewell's study cited in Chapter 1, if the returnees are equated by socioeconomic status.

As these four sources of information yielded some overlapping and corroborating data, gaps in one source could partly be filled by information from another. Nevertheless, about 15 percent of individual items of information are missing. Some of these, however, can be estimated (Chapter 4). In other instances, we had to reduce the number of Ex—C pairs being compared, lacking, as we were, essential information. In total, however, we believe that we obtained somewhere near the maximum possible data for a longitudinal study involving five research sites.

From these various sources of information we prepared a Dependent

Variable Index, using the following instructions for computing:

Combine scores on the following items, using positive sign when advantage is with the experimental child, negative sign when advantage is with the control child.

1. Persistence in School. (Score is determined by point difference between experimental and control subjects.)

   0. Tenth grade or less completed
   1. Eleventh grade completed
   2. Above eleventh grade, but not graduated from high school
   3. High school graduation
   4. Post-high school training (technical or vocational school)
   5. Junior or community college
   6. Four-year college or university
   7. Select four-year college or university

2. Special Track in High School.

   0. Less than half of school years after Special Opportunity Program in special track
   1. One-half or more of post-SOP years in special track

3. Special School.

   0. Not in special school after Special Opportunity Program
   1. In special (private or special academic) school

4. Achievement Tests.

   Where stanine scores are available, record difference in stanines.
   Where stanines are not available, use following measures:

   0. Less than half-year difference in achievement test scores
   1. One-half to .99 years difference
   2. One to 1.49 years difference
   3. 1.5 to 1.99 years difference
   4. 2.0 to 2.49 years difference

   (To match the possible range of stanines, that is, +8 to −8, this scale continues to maximum of 4.5 years difference; but in fact, only one pair showed more than 2.5 years contrast.)

5. Junior High School Grades (after the SOP), solid subjects.

   0. Less than .50 difference in average grade
   1. .50 to .99 difference
   2. 1.00 to 1.49 difference
   3. 1.50 or above average difference

6. Senior High School Grades, solid subjects (grades 10 through 12).

   (Calculate as in variable 5)

Table 2.10. *Outline of research design*

| | | Input variables[a] | Intervening variables | | Output variables[b] |
			Program and follow-up	Other intervening variables	
Matched	Experimental children	X	X	X	X
	Control children	X	O	X	X

[a] Tendencies and supportive opportunities of observed children.
[b] Levels of educational attainment.

Summary of procedures

In broadest outline, our research design compared educational attainment of experimental and control groups, matched as closely as possible. We included the quality of the match in the interpretations. In addition to the impact of the summer program and follow-up activities, we examined the effect of other intervening variables. Then, by multiple classification analysis and other statistical treatments, we indicated the sources of differences in the dependent variables: Persistence in School, Assignment to Special Track, Attendance at a Special School, Achievement Test scores, and Grades.

In schematic terms, then, our design was as shown in Table 2.10.

3. Backgrounds of the Middle Starters

Who were the children in the Special Opportunity Program? What resources did they bring to their educational experience? How much support could they count on from their families?

It was our aim to work with children who showed some promise of academic success as indicated by the usual measures, but who came from economically deprived neighborhoods and schools. We did not believe that our experimental stimulus would be strong enough or persist long enough to overcome extreme academic disadvantage. At the same time, if we selected only those who were already ahead of their peers (those whom teachers would have rewarded if we had asked them to nominate only their best), we could scarcely test our ability to modify academic performance. We wanted to see if careful encouragement of individual skills, motives, and aspirations, and of sociocultural support from school, family, and college could significantly alter the expected sequence of events. We sought, therefore, to select pupils with some po-

Table 3.1. *Distribution of pupils by year of participation, sex, and race*

Trait	Frequency by year			Total
	1964	1965	1966	
Sex				
Male	38	45	46	129
Female	18	25	23	66
Total	56	70	69	195
Ethnicity or racial group				
White	14	17	15	46
Mexican-American	1	3	—	4
Puerto Rican	3	3	4	10
Black	37	46	48	131
Mixed	1	1	1	3
American Indian	—	—	1	1

Table 3.2. *Cities from which pupils came*

City	Frequency by year			Total
	1964	1965	1966	
Cleveland	24	33	37	94
Elyria	6	7	5	18
Lorain	9	10	10	29
Oberlin	5	8	5	18
St. Louis	12	12	12	36

tential, but with academic and in some instances personal handicaps severe enough in many cases to call for special intervention if they were to go beyond high school. Their grades or their achievement scores were average or better, or they were recognized by their teachers as having undeveloped capacities, despite poor grades and achievement scores. The data in this chapter show the range of factors influencing the children in the experimental group as they entered the program.

The experimental group

Table 3.1 shows, by the year in which participants entered the program, their sex, and their race. As matters of policy, two-thirds of those chosen were male, two-thirds black, and we worked in cooperation with four school districts close to the campus and with the Banneker district of the St. Louis schools (Table 3.2). Almost all the pupils who first came to Oberlin were between the seventh and eighth grades; a few in the group of 1964 were between the eighth and ninth grades. Age of pupil shows a range from about twelve to fifteen years, with a mean of 160 months ($13\frac{1}{3}$ years); two-thirds were within four months, plus or minus, of thirteen years (Table 3.3). Thus most of the pupils were on schedule, as one would expect from the custom of automatic promotion through the grades in public schools.

Criteria for choosing experimental pupils

From among a large pool of disadvantaged pupils we sought those who had sufficient potential to overcome their handicap, if given help. The cooperating schools nominated pupils most of whose tested aptitude

Table 3.3. *Distribution of ages at time of entering program*

Age (in months)	Frequency by year			Total
	1964	1965	1966	
180—185	0	1	1	2
176—179	1	2	1	4
172—175	3	2	3	8
168—171	4	1	4	9
164—167	12	6	6	24
160—163	6	12	5	23
156—159	20	23	31	74
152—155	9	22	18	49
148—151	1	1	0	2
Total	56	70	69	195

Table 3.4. *Tested intelligence level at time of entry*

Intelligence score (stanines)	Frequency by year			Total
	1964	1965	1966	
9	3	3	2	8
8	21	11	4	36
7	17	19	17	53
6	11	25	23	59
5	4	9	14	27
4	—	1	7	8
3	—	2	2	4
2	—	—	—	—
1	—	—	—	—
Mean[a]	7.1	6.5	6.0	6.5
Standard deviation	1.0	1.3	1.3	1.3
N	56	70	69	195

[a]Mean stanines for the control group were 6.6, 6.2, and 6.1 for the three years, and 6.3 for the total. We take account of the small difference between control and experimental scores in our analysis.

and achievement scores ranged from average to superior, and whose traits — motivation, emotional and social maturity — seemed likely to reinforce talent and to respond to encouragement. To assess these latter

Table 3.5. *Mean grade-level scores on achievement tests at time of entry*

	1964	1965	1966	Total
Mean grade-level score	8.5	8.0	7.6	8.0
N	56	70	69	195

Table 3.6. *Mean class marks at time of entry (A = 4)*

	1964	1965	1966	Total
Seventh grade	2.8	2.7	2.7	2.7
N	56	70	69	195

traits we depended upon teachers' recommendations and similar testimonials. Aptitude and achievement scores were available from the regular batteries routinely administered throughout the pupils' careers in all the cooperating school districts.

To assess intelligence, many specific tests were used in varying combinations in the several districts: CTMM, WISC, Kuhlmann-Anderson, Pintner, Stanford-Binet, Lorge-Thorndike, Otis, Terman-McNemar, and the Cleveland Test of Probable Learning Rate being the major ones. Since scores were not directly interchangeable, they were converted to stanines, which show that most pupils were above average in tested intelligence (Table 3.4). This advantage takes on significance in the light of contemporary arguments, with which we agree (Chapter 2), that standard tests of intelligence systematically undermeasure pupils from lower-class backgrounds. But our pupils, recommended precisely because of such backgrounds, nonetheless showed strong potential. That the 1965 and 1966 groups had lower average scores than those of 1964 was a result of our request that more pupils in the lower range be nominated, because we wanted to assess the effects of the program on individuals who by these tests were of lesser "ability."

Similarly, average scores on achievement batteries and average class marks indicate success in finding disadvantaged students who were doing satisfactory or superior work, as well as participants of lower measured scores in the latter two years. Tables 3.5 and 3.6 show that the typical pupil rated better than average in academic aptitude, performed satisfactorily at grade or above on standard achievement tests, and had

Table 3.7. *Siblings in the home*

	Frequency by year			
Number of siblings	1964	1965	1966	Total
17	—	1	—	1
13	—	1	—	1
11	2	—	2	4
10	1	3	1	5
9	2	2	2	6
8	1	2	1	4
7	3	5	3	11
6	4	3	13	20
5	3	8	10	21
4	10	12	9	31
3	10	15	8	33
2	12	10	7	29
1	7	7	10	24
0	1	1	3	5
Total	56	70	69	195
Mean	3.9	4.2	4.2	4.1

attained marks averaging B−, when he entered the program. About one-fifth, however, fell below the average by the national or local norms we used, and another one-fifth tested as below average on one or another of the scales.

Home background

Although the home situation did not enter into the choosing of the experimental pupils, we used several dimensions of it as critical variables in interpreting our findings. Thus it is important to know the pupils' backgrounds. For one thing, the average pupil had more siblings than is usual (Table 3.7). Moreover, the parental pattern deviated from national norms; the homes were managed by the mother more often than is typical in other social and ethnic strata (Tables 3.8, 3.9). Twenty-nine percent of the families (57 out of 195) were without an adult male. Although precise comparisons are difficult to make, this proportion is high by national urban standards (10 to 15 percent) and similar to the urban black proportion, which was about 28 percent in 1968, the year

Table 3.8. *Father's status in the home*

	Frequency by year			
Father's status	1964	1965	1966	Total
Father in home	35	44	39	118
Stepfather in home	5	6	3	14
Other adult male in home	1	1	4	6
Father dead; no other adult male in home	0	2	2	4
Father alive, but not in home; no other adult male in home	15	17	19	51
Father unknown; no other adult male in home	0	0	2	2

Table 3.9. *Mother's status in the home*

	Frequency by year			
Mother's status	1964	1965	1966	Total
Mother in home	50	66	62	178
Stepmother in home	—	2	—	2
Other adult female in home	1	2	7	10
Mother dead; no other adult female in home	2	—	—	2
Mother not in home, but alive	3	—	—	3

when most of our family data were gathered (United States Department of Commerce, 1973: 68).

As to levels of parental education, we found important differences between fathers and mothers (Table 3.10). When the percentages shown in the last two columns are compared with 1969 data for the national population over twenty-five years of age we find, as expected, that the parents of our participants fall well below the national average. In the United States as a whole, 54 percent of both males and females have finished high school or gone further, compared with 37 percent and 41 percent in our sample. This contrast may, however, be misleading, because the age range of our parents is narrower than the national range and some data are missing, but these qualifications, if they have any effect, probably lead to underestimation of the differences.

Parental occupations are critical indicators of the disadvantaged

Table 3.10. Education of father and mother (frequency by year)

Highest level of schooling	1964		1965		1966		Total[a]	
	Father	Mother	Father	Mother	Father	Mother	Father	Mother
High school graduate or higher	16	18	14	29	19	28	49 (37)	75 (41)
9–11 years	11	23	18	26	14	23	43 (33)	72 (39)
5–8 years	9	7	18	12	8	11	35 (27)	30 (16)
0–4 years	2	1	1	2	2	4	5 (4)	7 (4)
Not applicable; or information lacking[b]	18	7	19	1	26	3	63	11

[a] Percentages (in parentheses) refer only to parents for whom information is available.
[b] This refers mainly to families without an adult male or female in the home.

Table 3.11. *Father's occupation*

Occupation	Frequency by year			Total[a]	
	1964	1965	1966		
Sales, clerical, managerial, professional	2	2	5	9	(6)
Skilled worker, foreman	10	10	9	29	(19)
Semiskilled, service, household worker	14	24	31	69	(46)
Laborer, farm laborer	12	22	8	42	(28)
Not applicable; or information lacking[b]	18	12	16	46	

[a] Percentages (in parentheses) refer only to fathers for whom information is available.
[b] This refers mainly to families without an adult male in the home.

Table 3.12. *Mother's occupation*

Occupation	Frequency by year			Total[a]	
	1964	1965	1966		
Sales, clerical, managerial, professional	5	5	6	16	(7)
Skilled worker, foreman	1	2	0	3	(2)
Housewife, laborer, service worker	45	62	60	167	(90)
Not applicable; or information lacking	5	1	3	9	

[a] Percentages (in parentheses) refer only to mothers for whom information is available.

backgrounds of program participants (Tables 3.11, 3.12). Again, it is difficult to compare these data with national standards, but as a rough guide we may note that 25 percent of the fathers of our participants were white-collar or skilled workers, whereas the national figure for all non-Whites was 37 percent in 1972 and for Whites it was 63 percent (United States Department of Commerce, 1973: 50). Because the mother was often both wage earner and home manager, we noted employment status as well as occupation (Table 3.13).

We were dealing, in brief, with a promising but disadvantaged group of pupils, many of whom would be expected, in the normal course of events, to complete their formal education at the age of sixteen and few

Table 3.13. *Mother's employment status*

	Frequency by year			Total[a]	
Employment status	1964	1965	1966		
Full-time employment	9	18	22	49	(27)
Part-time employment	2	0	2	4	(2)
Housewife	37	50	43	130	(71)
Not applicable; or information lacking	8	2	2	12	

[a] Percentages (in parentheses) refer only to mothers for whom information is available.

of whom would go on to college. Can those events be significantly altered by a fairly modest program — a program that could be widely duplicated where there is the will? Can early childhood deficits be overcome in early adolescence? Can there be a middle start?

4. Testing a hypothesis by matched pairs

Our research tests the following general hypothesis:

Among disadvantaged youths who have finished the seventh grade, an intensive but pleasant summer on a college campus, followed by long-term counseling, newsletters, reunion periods, supplemental academic training, conferences with parents, and other follow-up stimuli through the next several years, significantly affects academic performance, achievement test scores, and the likelihood of staying in school.

The research design by which we tested it is less commonly employed than designs appropriate to the small-group laboratory with its possibilities of elegant controls, or to the survey, with its possibilities of careful sampling even of national populations. Our design, however, has some important features in common with both. Like small-group laboratory research, ours is a true experiment; and like the survey, it is "in the field," a study of "real life" conditions (Drabek and Haas, 1967). This does not mean that we have the best of both worlds, for a field study that attempts a true experimental design faces difficulties of its own; yet it enjoys the great advantages of both realism and an experimental structure.

To some degree, approaches to the study of human behavior are reflections of what Robin Williams has called "types of scientific conscience":

To the historical and cultural conscience it is above all important that the object of study be historically and culturally important. . . . a conscience of this type would insist upon intimate familiarity with a wide range of materials, and place a high value on erudition.

To the "clinical" sociologist, on the other hand, a primary virtue is detailed and sensitive fidelity to the complex, immediate situation. His anxiety dreams are likely to be studded with horrid fancies of having "torn a fact out of context" or, perhaps worse, having "generalized beyond his data." His conscience is clear and his disposition sunny when after a long experience of immersion in a factory work group or a boy's gang he completes a vivid naturalistic description of complex behavior and its complex motivation. In his harsher moments, he may describe the historical or cultural sociologist as an "arm-chair theorist," the experiment as "artificial," and the survey as "crude" and "mechanical."

To persons in the logico-experimental group, the ideal study is the highly controlled experiment or the sample survey, complete with scales, scores, probability samples, and possibly electronic computers. (1958: 622–3)

Our scientific consciences led us closest to Williams' third type. By use of carefully matched experimental and control groups we undertook to test a causal hypothesis. At the same time, we hoped to maintain something of the clinical style by locating our facts in the context of school and community, and of the historical style by recognizing that the events we were studying are part of a major transformation of American society and cannot be understood outside of it.

Because our research took seven years in the field, we were confronted with experimental problems that are not as likely to disturb short-time laboratory research; but this was the price we paid for realism. We lost some respondents. We lacked a few items of information on one or both members of a matched pair. A longitudinal study faces the problem of "history," so that we had to ask: How much are observed changes the products of the program, how much the results of general developments in society or in the communities studied? This problem was aggravated by the fact that the historical forces are producing general tendencies similar to effects of our program. Ideally, comparison of the experimental and control groups should have permitted us to separate historical from experimental influences. This would have been possible, however, only if control and experimental pairs had been closely matched. In fact, almost every problem in a research design that employs a field study is reduced if close matching is possible. But precise matching is one of the most difficult tasks in field research. Many variables may affect the influence of the experimental stimulus, and must therefore be matched; theory may be insufficiently developed to identify the critical variables or their appropriate weighting; measurement of some variables is often imprecise; interaction effects are highly complex and not well understood; the pool from which both experimental and control groups must be drawn is often small; and randomization may be only partially available, or not at all.

Although problems of compensating for departures from ideal matching are common in sociological studies, even when experimental designs are used there is relatively little discussion of them.[1] In the laboratory a judicious combination of matching and randomization can often produce an approximation of the desired pattern. Various restraints on field research, however, may force deviation from the model, clouding interpretation of the results. Therefore in making our interpretation we used procedures (Chapter 2) that take account of the quality of the match.

Estimation of missing information

In the distributions of matching scores in each of the three years (using the ideal and directional indexes described in Chapter 2) it should be noted that some pairs in which information was lacking on one or both members were eliminated from the analysis (Tables 4.2, 4.3). In many cases, however, when only a few items were missing, we were able to estimate a score. There are at least three methods by which scores can be estimated:

First, a person for whom a measure is lacking can be assigned the midpoint of the range for that variable. Thus stanine 5 would be used, in variables 14 and 15 in the Index of Congruence (IQ and Achievement Tests), to estimate probable scores of those individuals for whom intelligence and achievement test scores were lacking. Or, where the score for a variable is directly comparative, as in item 2, the midpoint would be assigned to the pair without reference to individual measures. If we had no information on a pair or on a variable, this midpoint method of estimation would be reasonable, but as we do have information, other modes of estimation are wiser. We know that the midpoint is not the best estimate of the score of a variable with references to all those pairs on whom information is available. For example, when all but one pair has a score of 0 for variable 1, we would distort the matching picture if we assigned a score of 2 (the midpoint on variable 1) when, in fact, the mode is 0 and the mean score is less than .01

Problems associated with the first method of estimating missing scores lead to the second method, which is to assign to any pair for whom information on a variable is missing the mean score on that variable among all the pairs for whom information is complete. Thus if the mean contrast in "education of father" is .5, as calculated in variable 7, that score would be assigned to a pair for whom information is missing, rather than 2.0, which is the midpoint score. This procedure is based on the assumption that, in a relatively homogeneous group, known scores are a better indicator than is the midpoint of an arbitrary range.

The third method extrapolates from what is known about a given pair to fill in missing information. If, for example, we have data on fifteen variables for a pair, with an index of congruence of 16 points out of a possible total of 64, we can assign a score of 1 for the missing variable, which has a possible score of 4. In using the same ratio (1/4 : 16/64), we assume that existing information about a pair is the best source of estimation of missing data. This procedure treats the unmeasured variable neutrally, not letting it affect the observed relationship based on the measured variables, but rendering it unnecessary to remove a pair from the analysis because of the missing items.

For the most part we used the logic of the third method of data estimation, although, in fact, a more complicated and more powerful computer program was employed to identify similar profiles of scores among the full range of respondents. Clearly there are risks involved in any one of the procedures suggested; but in our judgment the third method is least likely to over- or underestimate the quality of the match.

The first step of the procedure was to identify clusters of variables, excluding all cases with missing value codes, where the variables in each cluster formed a single dimension. Guttman-Lingoes Multidimensional Scalogram Analysis One (MSA-1) was used for this purpose, with results as shown in Table 4.1.

Besides ascertaining the dimensionality of the clusters, the output of MSA-1 reports the different profile types found for each cluster of variables as well as the ID numbers of the cases belonging to each profile type. When, having determined four unidimensional clusters, we reran MSA-1 for each cluster, including a missing value code for each variable, profile types containing at least one missing data code were obtained.[2] Within each cluster, then, profile types containing full information were matched to each profile type containing missing codes. In a small number of cases, no profiles with full information were found to match, and consequently no estimates were obtained for the missing data profile. In addition, any profile type consisting of missing data for more than one half of the variables was discarded as containing too little information for purposes of estimation. Thus for each eligible profile with missing data a list of identical profiles with full information was obtained. By "identical" is meant identical scores on all variables contained in the incomplete profiles. Then for each subset of full-information profiles a frequency distribution was run for each variable on the missing data profile that contained a missing value code. The estimates of these

Table 4.1. *Variable clusters used in estimation procedure, with coefficients of contiguity*

Cluster	Coefficient of contiguity	Variables
1	.972	Father in the home
		Mother in the home
		Number of brothers
		Number of sisters
		Total number of siblings
		Birth order
2	.952	Number of years of school completed
		Special track or special school
		Junior High GPA
		Senior High GPA
3	.996	Age at time of program
		Sex
		Preprogram achievement test
		Preprogram IQ test
		Seventh grade GPA
4	.986	Father's occupation
		Father's education
		Mother's occupation
		Mother's education

missing value codes were taken to be the mean, median, or mode (dependent on the type of variable being estimated, i.e., interval, ordinal, or nominal) of this matched subsample. This procedure to establish appropriate subsamples was employed on all eligible profiles containing missing data in each of the four variable clusters.

It should be noted that this procedure has a slightly conservative effect, that is, it tends to reduce possible differences between the experimental and control groups. As data on the controls were somewhat less complete, they were more likely to be estimated. Scores for the experimental students on the dependent variables tended to be higher. Hence the process of estimating produced a smoothing out of the differences between experimentals and controls. Because overall, however, only 15 percent of the items were estimated in preparation of the Index of Congruence and less than 3 percent in preparation of the Dependent Variable Index, the leveling effect was not strong.

After the estimation procedures we were in a position to compare

Table 4.2. *Distribution of matching scores*

Range of difference between members of matched pairs in points[a]	Ideal index			
	1964	1965	1966	Total
2	0	1	1	2
3	0	2	1	3
4	0	0	2	2
5	2	4	2	8
6	1	5	2	8
7	3	8	3	14
8	5	2	5	12
9	5	5	3	13
10	1	5	4	10
11	4	3	3	10
12	3	2	3	8
13	1	3	2	6
14	1	0	6	7
15	2	2	2	6
16	0	1	1	2
17	5	4	4	13
18	1	1	3	5
19	1	2	0	3
20	0	1	0	1
21	0	1	2	3
22	1	0	0	1
23	2	0	0	2
24	1	0	1	2
N	39	52	50	141
Mean difference	12.38	10.23	11.52	11.28

[a] Total possible difference = 64.

the experimental and control groups as to their preprogram and postprogram scores. Table 4.2 indicates the range of difference scores between the experimental-control pairs before the program. A score of 0 would indicate identity, as measured on our sixteen variables in the In-

Table 4.3. *Average matching scores of fully matched pairs compared with scores of those incompletely matched, in percentages of deviation from a perfect match*

	1964	1965	1966	Total
Fully matched	19.34	15.98	18.00	17.60
Incompletely matched	20.07	18.18	18.60	18.87

dex of Congruence; a score of 64 would indicate maximum possible difference.

The 16-variable scale yielded matches that were imprecise when set against what we have called the ideal (Table 4.2). The average mismatch on the 64-point scale was 11.28 points (17.6 percent). Without some standard of comparison, we cannot say whether this is good or poor, and as the procedure is new there is no standard. It is our judgment, however, that in this kind of field research, with the inevitable constraints among five school systems, one could scarcely get average matching scores that fell below the obtained level.

Pairs were excluded from the tabulations of Table 4.2 if even one item of information was missing on either member of the pair, and could not be estimated. Does the exclusion of pairs that cannot be fully matched introduce a selective factor that makes the matching appear better or poorer than it was in the full set of pairs? We can give a reasonable answer to this question by converting the points of difference between matched pairs in Table 4.2 to percentage differences (percentage of the total possible 64 points) and comparing those differences with the percentage differences of the full set of 195 pairs. For fifty-four of the pairs a percentage was used based on something less than 64 points, because one or more items of information were lacking and could not be estimated. The fully matched pairs seem to be slightly more similar than those incompletely matched, but the difference is small (Table 4.3).

Using the Directional Matching Index, we find greater similarity between the sets of matched partners than was shown by the Ideal Index, for in the Directional Index a preprogram advantage held by one member of a pair might be balanced by a different advantage in the partner (Table 4.4). Here the N's are somewhat reduced because we have taken advantage of the estimation process and of the factor analysis of the variables in the Directional Index. Possible scores range from +16 (advantage to the experimental pupil) to −16 (advantage to the control pu-

Table 4.4. *Distribution of matching scores, Directional Index*

	1964	1965	1966	Total
+4	0	0	0	0
+3	0	2	1	3
+2	2	3	2	7
+1	18	10	16	44
0	6	19	12	37
−1	7	12	13	32
−2	3	2	4	9
−3	2	2	2	6
−4	1	2	0	3
N	39	52	50	141
Mean difference	−.03	−.15	−.08	−.09

pil), but actual differences are much smaller. By these measures, fifty-four of the experimental partners and fifty of the control partners have a preprogram advantage, and thirty-seven of the pairs are equal. The advantage is slightly greater in the control group on the average, hence there is a small mean difference in their favor.

Although Table 4.2 shows that the matches, using the sixteen variables of the Ideal Index, are somewhat imprecise, Table 4.4 shows, as we expected, that there is no large advantage to either experimental or control group when the Directional Index is used. Employing those criteria (family support and preprogram tests and grades) that we assume would give a pupil an advantage (see the discussion of the Directional Matching Index in Chapter 2), we find that the control group is slightly better off; but the advantage is small. The correlation between the ideal matching score and the directional matching score is very low (.03) indicating that randomization produced groups of nearly equal potential for academic success.

We are primarily interested in comparing individual pairs, however, and not group means; hence it is important to know the average distance from parity, disregarding signs. The average advantage of one or the other of the members of a pair was as follows: 1964 = 1.15; 1965 = 1.00; 1966 = 1.00; total = 1.04. These differences are based on a maximum advantage score of 4.0.

Effect of the program on academic achievement

These measures of initial advantage or equality must be compared with measures of achievement following our program. Six such measures, or dependent variables, were used, sometimes separately, sometimes together in a single index (maximum weights for each variable are given in parentheses):

Persistence in School (6)

Assignment to Special Track (1)

Admitted to Special School (1)

Achievement Test scores (stanine differences, where available, with a maximum possible contrast of 8, but with an empirical range of 4; and where stanines were not available, test-years, with each half-year contrast equaling one point)

Junior High School Grades (3)

Senior High School Grades (3)

Without reference to initial advantage of one or the other member of a pair, when all dependent variables were combined, the experimental partners showed higher scores than their control partners at a ratio of slightly more than two to one — 116 : 56 (Table 4.5). Sixteen of the pairs had identical scores. The size of the advantage was also greater for the experimental students, who enjoyed an average scale-step advantage of 4.8, compared with 3.5 among the control partners who were ahead.

This picture was only slightly changed when the factor analytic scores were used to indicate the extent of postprogram advantage. Because the theoretically possible difference was reduced from 22 to 4, the pairs showing no difference increased from 16 to 49 (Table 4.6). An advantage was shown by 92 experimental partners, compared with 53 control partners.

Starting with the general comparisons found in Tables 4.5 and 4.6, we may examine our experimental and control groups in several ways, using the six postprogram variables separately. First, we compare the 195 pupils who participated in the program as a group with the 195 controls. Still disregarding possible preprogram advantage to one or the other group, we assume that the matching process plus randomization produced near equivalence. Later we divide the groups by race and sex, take any preprogram differences into account, and apply various controls. The assumption of near equivalence proves to be correct, as we shall see, and the application of controls only slightly modifies the sig-

Table 4.5. *Comparison of postprogram achievement levels of matched pairs*

Dependent Variable Index	N	
11	3	
10	3	
9	4	
8	11	Total positive (experimental advantage) = 551 steps
7	13	
6	11	
5	9	Mean no. of scale steps advantage = 4.8
4	17	
3	14	
2	11	Number of individuals = 116
1	20	
0	16	
−1	11	
−2	12	Total negative (control advantage) = 193 steps
−3	8	
−4	11	
−5	5	Mean no. of scale steps advantage = 3.5
−6	2	
−7	4	
−8	2	Number of individuals = 56
−9	1	

Table 4.6. *Comparison of postprogram achievement levels of matched pairs (using factor analysis)*

Dependent Variable Factor Index	N	
4	5	Total positive = 178 steps
3	22	Mean number of scale steps = 1.9
2	27	
1	38	Number of individuals = 92
0	49	
−1	27	Total negative = 94 steps
−2	15	Mean number of scale steps = 1.8
−3	7	
−4	4	Number of individuals = 53

Table 4.7. Comparison of postprogram achievement levels of experimental and control groups

	N	Mean	Standard deviation	Standard error	T-value	2-tailed probability[a]
1. Persistence in School						
Experimentals	195	2.81	1.81	.132	1.17	+n.s.[b]
Controls	195	2.61	1.52	.113		
2. Assignment to Special Track						
Experimentals	195	.50	.50	.036	3.88	.001
Controls	195	.31	.46	.033		
3. Admitted to Special School						
Experimentals	195	.06	.24	.017	1.45	+n.s.[b]
Controls	195	.03	.17	.012		
4. Postprogram Achievement Tests						
Experimentals	195	5.81	2.03	.145	2.41	.016
Controls	194	5.34	1.80	.129		
5. Junior High Grades						
Experimentals	195	2.55	.81	.056	3.56	.001
Controls	194	2.27	.75	.054		
6. Senior High Grades						
Experimentals	195	2.23	.83	.059	2.63	.009
Controls	194	2.00	.85	.061		

[a]We might have used a one-tailed test, because we are making not only a prediction of difference but also one of direction. As a conservative measure, however, we have adopted the more demanding two-tailed test.

[b]+n.s. = not significant, but advantage to the experimental group.

nificance of the differences between experimentals and controls.

In four of the six dependent variables the experimental group has a significant advantage, with probabilities of .02 or less that the differences could be due to chance (Table 4.7). The persistence measure, although it does not show a significant difference, approaches significance for the 1964 cohort (see Appendix B). Insufficient time had elapsed to fully test this variable because most students, both control and experimental, finished high school. The third measure, Admitted to Special School, involved only 18 of the total of 390 individuals. Why were so few pupils attending special schools? The chief reason is that they are usually private and very expensive; only rarely did black or other minority pupils attend them. The few who did so were the beneficiaries of national scholarship campaigns to broaden the range of families served by private schools. Our intervention program did not emphasize special schools, because one of our basic aims was to use only the strategies generally available to public schools. Nonetheless, the tendency was in the predicted direction: twelve of the eighteen pupils came from the experimental group.

As noted in Table 4.7, we chose the two-tailed probability test, even though the one-tailed test would have been permissible. We wanted to be conservative, because the six measures reported are the crucial dependent variables. Even with this conservative test the most dependable T-values are striking. We suspect that Assignment to Special Track and Junior High Grades (variables 2 and 5 in Table 4.7) are the highest ranking because in the immediately preceding summer program heavy emphasis was laid upon junior high school experiences that were imminent. If the typical cycle of apathy were to be broken, the momentum would have to be maintained uninterrupted after the summer of our intervention. The T-values in Table 4.7 probably document the conscious effort made to capitalize on junior high school opportunities. Yet the other variables, reflecting the longer span of time through high school and into college, also show advantage to the experimental pupils.

Advantage scores within subgroups

The figures in Table 4.7 are for the total groups, indicating that the program had a significant effect. But they may disguise important internal variations where some subgroups were substantially influenced while others were not. Of several possible subdivisions those by race and sex seem most important. That these subgroups are small makes it less likely that differences will be significant. To aid interpretation, we divided the total groups in various ways, to estimate whether changes in probability resulted from size of sample or influence of program.

In Table 4.8 we made comparisons by race and sex separately to minimize sample shrinkage, and found in all twenty of the comparisons that, as expected, the advantage went to the experimental group. (We omitted the variable Admitted to Special School because so few pupils were involved.) Of the 20, 9 are significant at a p of .05 or higher, 3 others at .10 or higher, and the remaining 8 have p values above .10 (+n.s.). The number of significant differences varies directly with the size of the subgroup, so we conclude that size of sample, more than differential effects of the program, accounts for the variation.

When the total groups are considered by sex and race simultaneously, 19 of the 20 possible comparisons continue to favor the experimentals, 5 having p values of .05 or higher and 4 of .10 or higher, the remaining 11 having p values above .10, 10 being positive and 1 negative. When various controls are applied, this negative is eliminated, and a different one appears, as we shall see (Table 4.15), and there are other small shifts (Table 4.9).

As nearly half of our students were black males, we compared them with all the others, thus keeping larger samples (Table 4.10). Again all the comparisons are in the expected direction, favoring the experimental group. Of 10 comparisons, 5 are significant at the .05 level, 2 at the .10 level, and the remaining 3 not significant but with a positive sign. On two of the five variables, the black males show a greater advantage over their controls than do the other participants; Achievement Test scores, on the other hand, are significantly increased only among the latter.

Advantage scores compared with preprogram measures

Although preprogram measures showed no significant advantage to the experimental or control *groups,* there were advantages to individuals. We cannot fully test the influence of the program until we consider these initial advantages to one or another child in a matched pair. It can be done in a variety of ways. The Directional Index is correlated, as expected, with the Dependent Variable Index. Those partners, whether experimental or control, who started out with an advantage were likely

Table 4.8. *Probability that differences between experimentals and controls are significant, by sex and race*

| | N | Dependent variables[a] | | | | |
		Persistence in School	Assignment to Special Track	Achievement Tests	Jr. High Grades	Sr. High Grades
Male	189	+n.s.	+.002	+.089	+.001	+.018
Female	92	+n.s.	+.028	+.066	+n.s.	+n.s.
Black	192	+n.s.	+.004	+n.s.	+.002	+.009
Non-Black	89	+n.s.	+.009	+.026	+.096	+n.s.

[a] (+) = advantage to the experimental group.

Table 4.9. *Probability that differences between experimentals and controls are significant, by sex and race used simultaneously*

| | N | Dependent variables[a] | | | | |
		Persistence in School	Assignment to Special Track	Achievement Tests	Jr. High Grades	Sr. High Grades
Black male	135	+n.s.	+.066	+n.s.	+.005	+.046
Nonblack male	54	+n.s.	+.004	+.079	+.035	+n.s.
Black female	57	+n.s.	+.019	+n.s.	+.098	+.070
Nonblack female	35	+n.s.	+n.s.	+n.s.	+n.s.	−n.s.

[a] (+) = advantage to the experimental group; (−) = advantage to the control group.

Table 4.10. *Probability that differences between experimentals and controls on postprogram measures are significant, black males compared with all others*

	N	Dependent variables[a]				
		Persistence in School	Assignment to Special Track	Achievement Tests	Jr. High Grades	Sr. High Grades
Black males	135	+n.s.	+.066	+n.s.	+.005	+.046
All others	146	+n.s.	+.001	+.010	+.021	+.075

[a] (+) = advantage to the experimental group.

Table 4.11. *Shift of advantage score as a result of the program*

	Experimental group		Control group		Total
	0	e	0	e	
Before	66	77.5	74	62.5	140
	0	e	0	e	
After	89	77.5	51	62.5	140
Total	155		125		280

χ^2 = 6.995 (corrected for continuity), p = <.01, d.f. = 1

to end with an advantage. The correlations, however, are quite low: .36 when we use the original Directional Matching Index and Dependent Variable Index, and .17 when we use the factor scoring for the two variables. Thus only a small part of the variance in postprogram achievement measures (3 percent to 13 percent, depending on method of scoring) can be accounted for by preprogram advantages. (Such preprogram advantages will be controlled in the section on Multiple Classification Analysis at the end of this chapter.)

Additional calculations may indicate the shifts in advantage score from those originally recorded to those found after the program. The balance of shifts significantly favors the experimental group. Using the 140 pairs for whom we have complete preprogram and postprogram scores, we can examine the extent of the shift between the two measures. Before the program, seventy-four control pupils had scores on the Directional Index either equal to or superior to those of their experimental pairs, but the number dropped to fifty-one when the Dependent Variable Index was used as a measure of postprogram advantage. Table 4.11 applies the chi-square test to the null hypothesis: The distribution of advantage scores did not shift significantly as a result of the program; the number of control partners and experimental partners who had scored a higher advantage at Time One (before the program) did not differ significantly from the number at Time Two (after the program).

The null hypothesis is refuted; by the chi-square test the experimental subjects significantly improved their position on the index of Academic Achievement. The chi-square test, using dichotomous variables, may hide variations within each quadrant however, even though the total relationship significantly favors the experimental group. As a fur-

Table 4.12. *Preprogram to postprogram gain or loss in academic performance between matched pairs*

Advantage score on dependent variable
(Academic Achievement) index

		+2	+1	0	−1	−2	Total
	+2	8	5	0	0	1	14
	+1	6	17	4	6	0	33
Advantage score on Directional Index	0	13	21	15	12	4	65
	−1	4	3	5	5	1	18
	−2	0	3	3	3	1	10
	Total	31	49	27	26	7	140

ther test, therefore, we may break down the independent variable (original advantage from family background, preprogram test scores, and school performance) and the dependent variable (postprogram levels of achievement) into more refined categories. Table 4.12 shows steps of gain or loss compared with those of the partner, the maximum being +4 or −4, with positive numbers indicating a gain for the experimental pupil and negative numbers a gain for the control. (Because there are few extreme scores, we have compressed the scales into the range of +2 to −2.)

The diagonal scores (in boldface type) indicate the pairs that did not change in relationship to one another. In the lower right, for example, one control child started out with a two-step advantage over his partner and retains, by our measures, a two-step advantage. Each cell can be assigned a "score" by reference to the two indexes. Thus in the −1 and +2 cell on the lower left there are four pairs where the experimental pupil started out with a one-step disadvantage (−1), but later held a two-step advantage (+2), a gain of three steps.

Whether we cite the number of individuals who improved their position or the number of steps by which positions were improved, the results match those of the chi-square test. They also reveal small additional gains by some experimental pupils that were obscured in the 2 ×

Table 4.13. *Preprogram to postprogram gain or loss in academic performance between matched pairs, using factor scores*

Advantage score on dependent variable
(Academic Achievement) index

		+2	+1	0	−1	−2	Total
	+2	2	2	3	1	1	9
	+1	17	9	8	4	6	44
Advantage score on	0	11	8	9	7	2	37
Directional Index	−1	5	6	11	4	6	32
	−2	2	5	7	1	3	18
	Total	37	30	38	17	18	140

2 table. In Table 4.12 there was no change in the relative scores of 46 pairs; in 61 pairs the experimentals gained a total of 94 scale steps; and 33 of the controls a total of 46 scale steps. That is, 44 percent of the experimentals gained, 33 percent held their own, and 24 percent lost, with initial level of advantage or disadvantage taken into account.

When the factor variables are used for both the preprogram Directional Index and the Dependent Variable Index, the results are very similar to those obtained by using the original variables (Table 4.13). The only important change is a reduction of the number of pairs in which one or the other partner did not show a gain. Pairs falling along the diagonal were reduced from 46 to 27. Of the 19 who shifted, 12 show an advantage to the experimental partner, 7 to the control partner − close to the ratio of advantage of the total series. The factor scores show that 73 (52 percent) of the experimental pupils gained, 27 (19 percent) of the pairs did not change, and 40 (29 percent) of the controls gained (initial level of advantage or disadvantage being taken into account). The experimental partners gained a total of 123 scale steps and the control partners 66 scale steps, an average of 1.68 steps for the former and 1.65 for the latter.

Various correlations can help us to interpret further the effects of the program. As noted in the section on estimation of missing information earlier in this chapter, we estimated information missing from a variable by assigning to it the average value found among those respondents whose scores on other variables matched those of the individual with the missing score. Did this estimation produce an apparent effect of the program where there really was no such effect? Or did it hide effects that in fact existed? We think not. The higher the number of estimated items (that is, the less complete the information), the lower the scores on both the Dependent Variable Index and the Dependent Variable Factor Index, indicating that scantier information was correlated with advantage to the control partner. Both correlations were low, however ($-.10$ for the Dependent Variable Index and $-.06$ for the Dependent Variable Factor Index), and insignificant. Insofar as the estimation procedure had any effect, it raised the postprogram scores of the control group. Advantage to the experimental pupil is not a function of meager information.

Tables 4.12 and 4.13 show that the postprogram advantage scores of the experimental group are not a function of preprogram advantages when the Directional Index is used. This issue can be examined further by using the Ideal Index of preprogram advantages in both the original form and the modified form using factor scores. There are small correlations between matching scores on the Ideal Index and the Ideal Factor Index, on one hand — these indicate closeness of match, not amount of information — and the Dependent Variable and Dependent Variable Factor Indexes, on the other: $r = .14$ for the former and $.03$ for the latter. That is, the more unlike the members of a pair were to begin with —without specifying either child, because we are referring here to the Ideal, not the Directional Index — the more probable it was that the experimental pupil would show an advantage after the program. Reverting to Figure 2.2, we note that the regression line, although much closer to line B than to line A, is not quite horizontal. However, the correlations are not significantly above zero, although the larger correlation ($r = .14$) approaches significance ($p = .09$).

Multiple Classification Analysis

So far the measures used support the hypothesis we stated at the beginning of this chapter. This support is limited, however, because of various problems inherent in those measures. In some cases, interpretations are limited by size of sample which, in turn, is held down by the application of controls. In others, we assumed that matching and random assignment produced equivalent experimental and control pupils. And we disregarded the cities from which the participants came and the years in which the students took part in the program. In order to provide a more rigorous test of the impact of the program, we analyzed the data by a technique — Multiple Classification Analysis (MCA) — that permits examination of postprogram differences between the experimentals and the controls, while simultaneously controlling for or partialling out any effects attributable to preprogram matching differences, sex, race, city, and year.

In general, MCA is a multivariate technique to examine the relationship between a predictor (independent) variable and a dependent variable by holding constant the effects of other predictors (e.g., the relationship between treatment condition and Persistence in School, while controlling preprogram match, sex, race, city, and year). When multiple predictors are so used, MCA yields a net or adjusted score equivalent to the mean value of the dependent variable for each category of a given predictor, after controlling the effects of the remaining predictors. The MCA program also gives a beta coefficient that can be used in a comparative manner to assess variation in the impact of the program among the several dependent variables, after the effects of the other predictor variables have been partialled out. Further calculations yield an associated F-test ($F_{[net]}$) that can determine whether one predictor explains a significant proportion of the variance in the dependent variable, other predictors being held constant. Although in principle MCA resembles multiple regression and analysis of variance, it has three distinct advantages over them: unlike regression analysis, it puts no restriction on the nature of the predictor variables, which may be entered in interval, ordinal, or nominal form; unlike analysis of variance, it allows correlation among the predictors; and statistical controls base the adjusted or net scores on the total sample rather than on the much smaller subsamples (Andrews, Morgan, and Sonquist, 1967). The N here (281) differs from the total N of 390 because we excluded cases where missing information could not be estimated by our procedures. Home city and year of participation in the program were introduced as control variables. School policies and environments varied somewhat among the cities; and the summer programs, despite similar basic formats, were not identical in staff, student makeup, or range of activities. The impact of the stimulus, therefore, might vary among pupils from different schools and at different times; hence city and year were taken into account.

Briefly stated, the findings are that even after preprogram differences

Table 4.14. *Multiple Classification Analysis of the net effects[a] of treatment condition on postprogram achievement levels*

Treatment condition	N	%	Net mean[b]	Beta	F(net)[c]
Persistence in School					
Experimentals	137	50.7	2.803		
Controls	133	49.3	2.579		
Total	270	100.0	2.693	.068	+n.s.
Assignment to Special Track					
Experimentals	141	50.2	.469		
Controls	140	49.8	.306		
Total	281	100.0	.388	.167	p<.01
Postprogram Achievement Tests					
Experimentals	141	50.2	5.981		
Controls	140	49.8	5.377		
Total	281	100.0	5.680	.151	p<.001
Junior High Grades					
Experimentals	141	50.2	2.56		
Controls	140	49.8	2.27		
Total	281	100.0	2.42	.189	p<.001
Senior High Grades					
Experimentals	141	50.2	2.24		
Controls	140	49.8	2.00		
Total	281	100.0	2.13	.149	p<.01

[a] Controlling preprogram match, sex, race, city, and year.
[b] See Chapter 2 for explanation of scoring of these variables in Tables 4.14–4.22.
[c] (+) = advantage to the experimental group.

(that is, advantage to the experimental or control group), sex, race, city, and year are controlled, the experimental and control students differ in the predicted direction on all dependent variables (Table 4.14). The experimentals are more likely to stay in school longer, to be assigned to a special academic track, to score higher on achievement tests and to have higher junior and senior high school grade-point averages. Furthermore, by the F-test for net effects most differences are significant at the .05 level or higher.

Although statistically significant, none of these effects is large. We did not suppose that an educational program — a modest one at that — could alone offset the influence of the larger environment's discrimination and limited opportunities (Rainwater, 1970). Nor did we expect that limited stimulation would cancel out the preprogram advantages some students had over others, particularly as measured by school performance and parental status. Yet the program did make a difference: pupils in the experimental group attained, on the average, one-third of a step on the persistence scale (two-thirds in the 1964 cohort); 47 percent spent half or more of their time in a higher track or in a special academic school (an opportunity which was not available in some of the school systems) compared to 31 percent of the control group; the experimentals exceeded the controls by a 0.6 stanine gain in achievement tests; and they attained junior and senior high grades of about one-third of a step higher (e.g., B— compared to C+).

To say that these were gains on the average does not give the full range of the facts. It is more precise to say with regard to Persistence in School, for example, that half of the experimental partners gained an average of a year over their controls, one-third held even, and one-sixth sustained an average loss of half a year, totaling an average gain of one-third of a year.

In analyzing postprogram scores, moreover, we need to see whether any gains are differentially distributed among various subgroups in the total sample, because use of the total groups may obscure larger gains among certain respondents while hiding smaller gains, or even losses, among others. This prompted us again to search for sources of variation in the impact of the program by race and sex after preprogram differences, city, and year were controlled (Tables 4.15 to 4.19).

Of the forty-five comparisons, forty-four are in the expected direction, experimental pupils showing a postprogram advantage over their control peers.[3] (The expected direction is reversed only in the case of Persistence in School among black females, as shown in Table 4.15.) Even with the smaller size of the subsamples, sixteen of these differences are significant at the .05 level or higher and an additional seven comparisons are significantly different at the .10 level.

When the group is divided, the beta coefficients show important differences among the subsamples on the several dependent variables. In regard to Persistence in School, the program seems to have had its greatest impact on black males and nonblack females, who attained the highest mean levels and surpassed their control partners by .31 and .61

Table 4.15. *Multiple Classification Analysis of the net effects of treatment condition on Persistence in School, on selected subsamples*

Treatment condition	N	%	Net mean	Beta	F(net)[d]
Males[a]					
Experimentals	93	51.1	2.905		
Controls	89	48.9	2.628		
Total	182	100.0	2.769	.087	+n.s.
Females[a]					
Experimentals	44	50.0	2.610		
Controls	44	50.0	2.458		
Total	88	100.0	2.534	.048	+n.s.
Blacks[b]					
Experimentals	95	51.1	2.844		
Controls	91	48.9	2.658		
Total	186	100.0	2.753	.054	+n.s.
Non-Blacks[b]					
Experimentals	42	50.0	2.721		
Controls	42	50.0	2.398		
Total	84	100.0	2.560	.112	+n.s.
Black males[c]					
Experimentals	67	51.1	3.031		
Controls	64	48.9	2.717		
Total	131	100.0	2.878	.090	+n.s.
Nonblack males[c]					
Experimentals	26	51.0	2.535		
Controls	25	49.0	2.444		
Total	51	100.0	2.490	.032	+n.s.
Black females[c]					
Experimentals	28	50.9	2.437		
Controls	27	49.1	2.472		
Total	55	100.0	2.454	.011	−n.s.
Nonblack females[c]					
Experimentals	16	48.5	2.981		
Controls	17	51.5	2.370		
Total	33	100.0	2.667	.208	+n.s
Black males[c]					
Experimentals	67	51.1	3.031		
Controls	64	48.9	2.717		
Total	131	100.0	2.878	.090	+n.s.

Table 4.15. (*cont.*)

Treatment condition	N	%	Net mean	Beta	F(net)[d]
All others[c]					
Experimentals	70	50.4	2.584		
Controls	69	49.6	2.451		
Total	139	100.0	2.518	.044	+n.s.

[a] Controlling preprogram match, race, city, and year.
[b] Controlling preprogram match, sex, city, and year.
[c] Controlling preprogram match, city, and year.
[d] (+) = advantage to the experimental group; (−) = advantage to the control group.

scale steps respectively — differences which, however, are not statistically significant. Its lowest impact was on black females and nonblack males, with a nonsignificant but negative score in the former comparison.

Although the experimental students are not significantly different from the controls in the persistence variable, all comparisons, for the total group and each subgroup, are in the predicted direction. When year of participation is taken into account, moreover, influence of the program is clearly shown. Persons in the last cohort (1966) were still in high school at the time of the last complete measure of persistence, which left little room for differentiation, as a majority of both control and experimental groups finish high school. Differentiation begins with the 1965 group, most of whom were seniors, but some of whom were, potentially, in the first year of college at the time of the last measure, while those in the 1964 cohort could have been sophomores. Experimentals of the 1964 group were, on the average, more than two-thirds of a scale-step ahead of their control partners. Although this does not quite attain statistical significance, the difference (Table 4.16) is in contrast to the virtual equality of control and experimental students in the 1966 cohort (see also Appendix B).

On Assignment to a Special Track (Table 4.17), the greatest effect of the program is on black females, but it appears to have had very little impact on nonblack females. This reverses the situation on the persistence variable. The experimentals show an advantage among both black and nonblack males. Although the difference is slightly larger in the latter group, it does not reach statistical significance because of sample size.

The influence of the program on Achievement Tests seems to be es-

Table 4.16. *Multiple Classification Analysis of the net effects of treatment condition on Persistence in School, by year of participation*

Year of participation	N	%	Net mean	Beta	$F(net)^a$
1964					
Experimentals	37	48.7	4.520		
Controls	39	51.3	3.840	.183	+n.s.
1965					
Experimentals	51	51.0	2.850		
Controls	49	49.0	2.790	.037	+n.s.
1966					
Experimentals	49	52.1	1.363		
Controls	45	47.9	1.360	.002	+n.s.

[a](+) = advantage to the experimental group.

Table 4.17. *Multiple Classification Analysis of the net effects of treatment condition on Assignment to Special Track, on selected subsamples*

Treatment condition	N	%	Net mean	Beta	$F(net)^d$
Males[a]					
Experimentals	96	50.8	.447		
Controls	93	49.2	.291		
Total	189	100.0	.370	.162	p<.05
Females[a]					
Experimentals	45	48.9	.515		
Controls	47	51.1	.336		
Total	92	100.0	.424	.181	p<.10
Blacks[b]					
Experimentals	96	50.0	.473		
Controls	96	50.0	.297		
Total	192	100.0	.385	.181	p<.01
Non-Blacks[b]					
Experimentals	45	50.6	.472		
Controls	44	49.4	.312		
Total	89	100.0	.393	.164	+n.s.
Black males[c]					
Experimentals	68	50.4	.427		
Controls	67	49.6	.283		
Total	135	100.0	.356	.151	p<.10

Table 4.17. (*cont.*)

Treatment condition	N	%	Net mean	Beta	$F(net)^d$
Nonblack males[c]					
Experimentals	28	51.9	.488		
Controls	26	48.1	.321		
Total	54	100.0	.407	.170	+n.s.
Black females[c]					
Experimentals	28	49.1	.596		
Controls	29	50.9	.321		
Total	57	100.0	.456	.276	p<.05
Nonblack females[c]					
Experimentals	17	48.6	.407		
Controls	18	51.4	.338		
Total	35	100.0	.371	.071	+n.s.
Black males[c]					
Experimentals	68	50.4	.427		
Controls	67	49.6	.283		
Total	135	100.0	.356	.151	p<.10
All others[c]					
Experimentals	73	50.0	.507		
Controls	73	50.0	.329		
Total	146	100.0	.418	.181	p<.05

[a] Controlling preprogram match, race, city, and year.
[b] Controlling preprogram match, sex, city, and year.
[c] Controlling preprogram match, city, and year.
[d] (+) = advantage to the experimental group.

pecially strong among nonblack females and weak among black males (Table 4.18). Expressed in terms of stanine differences between experimental and control groups (in each instance in favor of the experimental), the comparisons are: nonblack females 1.24; nonblack males .95; black females .85; black males .26. As achievement test measures, being based on national norms, are not strongly influenced by local measurement problems, these differences are particularly noteworthy.

In Junior High Grades there do not seem to be any large differences among the several subsamples (Table 4.19). Perhaps the slightly larger gains in the two male groups are influenced by the fact that they start from a lower base. Although only black males show a significant difference, all four race—sex differences are in the expected direction.

Table 4.18. *Multiple Classification Analysis of the net effects of treatment condition on postprogram Achievement Tests, on selected subsamples*

Treatment condition	N	%	Net mean	Beta	F(net)[d]
Males[a]					
Experimentals	96	50.8	5.809		
Controls	93	49.2	5.358		
Total	189	100.0	5.587	.111	p<.001
Females[a]					
Experimentals	45	48.9	6.341		
Controls	47	51.1	5.418		
Total	92	100.0	5.870	.239	p<.01
Blacks[b]					
Experimentals	96	50.0	5.631		
Controls	96	50.0	5.192		
Total	192	100.0	5.411	.108	p<.10
Non-Blacks[b]					
Experimentals	45	50.6	6.755		
Controls	44	49.4	5.751		
Total	89	100.0	6.258	.284	p<.001
Black males[c]					
Experimentals	68	50.4	5.462		
Controls	67	49.6	5.203		
Total	135	100.0	5.333	.064	+n.s.
Nonblack males[c]					
Experimentals	28	51.9	6.680		
Controls	26	48.1	5.730		
Total	54	100.0	6.222	.251	p<.05
Black females[c]					
Experimentals	28	49.1	6.029		
Controls	29	50.9	5.179		
Total	57	100.0	5.596	.204	p<.10
Nonblack females[c]					
Experimentals	17	48.6	6.841		
Controls	18	51.4	5.817		
Total	35	100.0	6.314	.327	p<.05
Black males[c]					
Experimentals	68	50.4	5.462		
Controls	67	49.6	5.203		
Total	135	100.0	5.333	.064	+n.s.

Table 4.18. (*cont.*)

Treatment condition	N	%	Net mean	Beta	$F(net)^d$
All others[c]					
Experimentals	73	50.0	6.473		
Controls	73	50.0	5.526		
Total	146	100.0	6.000	.247	p<.001

[a] Controlling preprogram match, race, city, and year.
[b] Controlling preprogram match, sex, city, and year.
[c] Controlling preprogram match, city, and year.
[d] (+) = advantage to the experimental group.

Table 4.19. *Multiple Classification Analysis of the net effects of treatment condition on Junior High Grades, on selected subsamples*

Treatment condition	N	%	Net mean	Beta	$F(net)^d$
Males[a]					
Experimentals	96	50.8	2.47		
Controls	93	49.2	2.15		
Total	189	100.0	2.31	.203	p<.01
Females[a]					
Experimentals	45	48.9	2.77		
Controls	47	51.1	2.53		
Total	92	100.0	2.65	.174	p<.10
Blacks[b]					
Experimentals	96	50.0	2.54		
Controls	96	50.0	2.24		
Total	192	100.0	2.39	,197	p<.01
Non-Blacks[b]					
Experimentals	45	50.6	2.63		
Controls	44	49.4	2.32		
Total	89	100.0	2.48	.194	p<.10
Black males[c]					
Experimentals	68	50.4	2.44		
Controls	67	49.6	2.13		
Total	135	100.0	2.29	.206	p<.05

Table 4.19. (*cont.*)

Treatment condition	N	%	Net mean	Beta	$F(net)^d$
Nonblack males[c]					
Experimentals	28	51.9	2.51		
Controls	26	48.1	2.21		
Total	54	100.0	2.36	.180	+n.s.
Black females[c]					
Experimentals	28	49.1	2.78		
Controls	29	50.9	2.51		
Total	57	100.0	2.64	.200	+n.s.
Nonblack females[c]					
Experimentals	17	48.6	2.78		
Controls	18	51.4	2.54		
Total	35	100.0	2.66	.176	+n.s.
Black males[c]					
Experimentals	68	50.4	2.44		
Controls	67	49.6	2.13		
Total	135	100.0	2.29	.206	p<.05
All others[c]					
Experimentals	73	50.0	2.67		
Controls	73	50.0	2.41		
Total	146	100.0	2.54	.173	p<.05

[a] Controlling preprogram match, race, city, and year.
[b] Controlling preprogram match, sex, city, and year.
[c] Controlling preprogram match, city, and year.
[d] (+) = advantage to the experimental group.

Finally, in Senior High Grades, the major source of variation among the subsamples appears to be the small effect of the program on non-black females (Table 4.20). In the other three race–sex groups, gains of experimental students in Senior High Grades are virtually the same as those in Junior High Grades.

The effects of the controls, quality of preprogram match, city, and year, are small (Tables 4.15–4.20). That is, the pattern of differences revealed in Table 4.9, where those controls were not used, is not greatly dissimilar. Comparing the equivalent lines in those tables, where race and sex are controlled simultaneously, we can usefully summarize the

Table 4.20. *Multiple Classification Analysis of the net effects of treatment condition on Senior High Grades, on selected subsamples*

Treatment condition	N	%	Net mean	Beta	F(net)[d]
Males[a]					
Experimentals	96	50.8	2.12		
Controls	93	49.2	1.85		
Total	189	100.0	1.99	.171	p<.05
Females[a]					
Experimentals	45	48.9	2.50		
Controls	47	51.1	2.32		
Total	92	100.0	2.40	.113	+n.s.
Blacks[b]					
Experimentals	96	50.0	2.24		
Controls	96	50.0	1.97		
Total	192	100.0	2.11	.156	p<.05
Non-Blacks[b]					
Experimentals	45	50.6	2.28		
Controls	44	49.4	2.05		
Total	89	100.0	2.17	.146	+n.s.
Black males[c]					
Experimentals	68	50.4	2.13		
Controls	67	49.6	1.87		
Total	135	100.0	2.00	.160	p<.10
Nonblack males[c]					
Experimentals	28	51.9	2.11		
Controls	26	48.1	1.82		
Total	54	100.0	1.97	.179	+n.s.
Black females[c]					
Experimentals	28	49.1	2.50		
Controls	29	50.9	2.23		
Total	57	100.0	2.36	.158	+n.s.
Nonblack females[c]					
Experimentals	17	48.6	2.50		
Controls	18	51.4	2.45		
Total	35	100.0	2.47	.035	+n.s.
Black males[c]					
Experimentals	68	50.4	2.13		
Controls	67	49.6	1.87		
Total	135	100.0	2.00	.160	p<.10

Table 4.20. (*cont.*)

Treatment condition	N	%	Net mean	Beta	$F(net)^d$
All others[c]					
Experimentals	73	50.0	2.35		
Controls	73	50.0	2.14		
Total	146	100.0	2.24	.129	+n.s.

[a] Controlling preprogram match, race, city, and year.
[b] Controlling preprogram match, sex, city, and year.
[c] Controlling preprogram match, city, and year.
[d] (+) = advantage to the experimental group.

examination by MCA of the program's effects. Without the statistical controls, 19 out of 20 comparisons are to the advantage of the experimental subgroups, 5 being significant at the .05 level or higher, 4 at the .10 level, 10 nonsignificant but positive, and 1 nonsignificant and negative. With the statistical controls, 19 out of 20 comparisons are in the expected direction, with 4 significant at the .05 level or higher, 3 at the .10 level, 12 positive but not significantly, and 1 negative but not significantly.

This total comparison obscures some internal shifts. Levels of significance remained the same when controls were applied in 10 out of the 20 comparisons; they became more favorable to the experimental group in 4 cases and less favorable in 6. In all of these 6, advantage remained with the experimentals but at a lower level of significance. Of the 10 shifts, whether positive or negative, 7 were of one "step," e.g., from $p = $ +n.s. to $p = <.10$, or from $p = <.05$ to $p = <.10$. The smallness of the shifts indicates that they are random, as is expected with small samples. This interpretation also fits the fact that 5 of the 10 shifts occurred among the males, 5 among the females, 5 among Blacks, 5 among non-Blacks.

That using MCA only moderately changes the comparisons between experimental and control groups is strong evidence supporting the preprogram equivalence attained by their matching and random assignment. We are confident, therefore, that the differences in educational performance which favor the experimental group are indeed consequences of the program.

These multiple classification analyses are based on an additive model that, while adequate for testing the influence of the program, may

Table 4.21. *Multiple Classification Analysis of the net effects of treatment condition on Persistence in School, by level of IQ*

IQ level	N	%	Net mean	Beta	$F(net)^a$
Stanines 3−5					
Experimentals	28	47.5	2.26		
Controls	31	52.5	2.57	.096	−n.s.
Stanine 6					
Experimentals	42	48.8	2.68		
Controls	44	51.2	2.51	.055	+n.s.
Stanine 7					
Experimentals	40	50.0	3.08		
Controls	40	50.0	2.47	.170	<.05
Stanines 8−9					
Experimentals	27	60.0	3.17		
Controls	18	40.0	2.97	.057	+n.s.

^{a}(+) = advantage to the experimental group; (−) = advantage to the control group.

obscure various interactive effects. Although we do not undertake a systematic study of possible interactions, we will illustrate the way they can operate by examining the effects of IQ further. It is one thing to control IQ; it is something else to ask: Does the effect of the program differ on persons at different IQ levels, when race, sex, quality of match, city and year are controlled? To illustrate, we asked this question with reference to two of our dependent variables: Persistence in School and Junior High Grades. By consolidating stanines at the lower and upper ends, we divided our respondents approximately into quartiles for this comparison.

Some interaction effect appears between level of IQ and the experimental stimulus with regard to Persistence in School (Table 4.21). The program differentiated most strongly between controls and experimentals at the higher levels of IQ, significantly on the stanine 7 level. (Some kind of ceiling effect may be operating on the top quartile to prevent significant improvement.) These were the pupils best able to take advantage of the program and most responsive to its stimuli. A reversal of the predicted scores appeared among those of lower IQ, the controls showing greater persistence than the experimentals. The difference is not significant, but we should be aware of a possible "frog-pond" effect (Davis, 1966). Students with lower IQs may have been discouraged from going on in school by the experience of comparing themselves

Table 4.22. *Multiple Classification Analysis of the net effects of treatment condition on Junior High Grades, by level of IQ*

IQ level	N	%	Net mean	Beta	$F(net)^a$
Stanines 3—5					
Experimentals	29	47.5	2.30		
Controls	32	52.5	2.17	.098	+n.s.
Stanine 6					
Experimentals	43	47.8	2.61		
Controls	47	52.2	2.11	.325	<.01
Stanine 7					
Experimentals	41	49.4	2.56		
Controls	42	50.6	2.37	.125	+n.s.
Stanines 8—9					
Experimentals	28	59.6	2.80		
Controls	19	40.4	2.58	.192	+n.s.

^{a} (+) = advantage to the experimental group.

with the more capable participants — comparisons that were perhaps more direct and powerful in the close contacts of the summer program than in school. Not much should be made of this interpretation, however, because the differences were not significant and discouragement did not appear in the variable of Junior High Grades.

In the case of possible effects of interaction between IQ and the stimulus on Junior High Grades, again one of the four comparisons shows a significant advantage in the experimental group. Although all four comparisons are in the predicted direction, the experimental students in stanine 6 were most clearly distinguished from their matched controls in Junior High Grades.

Experimental students with lower IQ gained least vis-à-vis their partners, but the contrasts with other IQ levels are small. Experimental—control differences in mean Junior High Grades vary from .13 (stanines 3—5) to .50 (stanine 6). On this variable, although there is some hint in the data of a possible interaction between IQ and the stimulus, no decisive interaction is shown.

5. Toward educational enrichment

Having reviewed the data of the Middle Start program and analyzed some of the relationships in a moderately well-matched panel of 195 pairs of pupils from disadvantaged communities, we may now summarize our findings. Although neither experimental nor control group started with an advantage over the other as a result of imperfect matching — near-equivalence between groups having been obtained by random assignment — some *individuals* were ahead of their pair partners. Hence we took account of the quality of the match in our analysis.

Summary of empirical findings

The experimental group attained significantly higher scores than the control group on four postprogram measures of academic performance, supporting our hypothesis in each instance. A fifth measure was in the expected direction, but not to the level of statistical significance. A sixth measure that applied to less than 5 percent of the 390 pupils did not significantly differentiate experimental from control group, but it did favor the former, as we had hypothesized.

It is equally important to note the subgroup variations. In broadest terms, the black participants — particularly the males — were more influenced by the program than were the nonblacks; white males were least affected. The "same" experience was clearly not the same to children with different tendencies and benefiting from different patterns of group support (for a similar finding, see Porter, 1974). In our judgment, several factors produced the range of outcomes.

The program was a more decisive experience for the black males than for the others. The civil rights movement, which was then at its height, may well have produced a multiplier effect, increasing the impact of our intervention on the black males. At the same time, it appears to us that the program tended to discourage participants from joining the more extreme and isolationist groups agitating for equality. Although we do not have hard evidence on this, we believe, as a result of continuing contact and the observations of teachers and counselors, that students in the program are fully aware of and involved in civil rights issues, yet also have kept in contact with (across race lines), and have given mutual support to, their fellow participants in the program.

In the Special Opportunity Program some black pupils met for the first time skilled black teachers and counselors — who were well represented on our staff — in positions of authority. It was not a new experience for them to be in the numerical majority, but it had a different quality when many of their directors, master teachers, and college-age counselors were black, and just as competent as the ones who were white. Conversely, white participants might have felt less closely attached to the program because *they* were a minority. We have no evidence, but our measures and observations may have been insufficiently sensitive to record such feelings.

A recent study in Philadelphia, based on survey rather than experimental data, found a similar pattern (Summers and Wolfe, 1975: 16-17). Black pupils showed greater gains than nonblack in junior high schools where the former constituted 50 percent or more of the student body. This finding is based on a regression analysis that held constant the effect of school size, teacher preparation, proportion of high-achieving students, and other variables. As these variables are generally strongly influenced in the public schools by the ratios of black and nonblack pupils, effects of the black proportion as a distinctive variable are usually obscured.

Our findings and those of the Philadelphia study may show the effects of a sense of alienation among some working-class white Americans who are not sure that the main currents of change are helping them (Greeley, 1974). Our sample is too small to separate pupils of Spanish-speaking descent (mainly second- and third-generation Americans) from those of older American background. Nor can we, because our program antedated them, study the possible effects of more recent Brown Power or other ethnic trends. We assume, nevertheless, that a kind of heavy-hearted disillusionment, coming perhaps from family attitudes, may have affected our white subjects somewhat more than our black. Where opportunities for a student to move to a higher track or a special school presented themselves, a few white parents discouraged the shift, asking "What is to be gained?" — a response which suggests a lack of enthusiasm for education more often found among working-class white parents than among their black counterparts.[1]

We should not forget, however, that *all* groups were shown to be significantly influenced on some measures of performance, although some subgroups were too small for the results to reach statistical significance. For example, both black and nonblack males in the experimental group showed nearly the same advantage over their control partners in junior high marks: one-third of a step in each instance but, because the former group is more than twice as large, its advantage over the control group reached the .05 level of significance, while in the latter case the same amount of advantage was not significant.

Our analysis of the subgroups shows which deficits can be overcome by our kind of program. Black males were significantly more likely to improve in terms of Grades, especially in junior high, although they made only a moderate and nonsignificant improvement in Achievement Test scores. We think that the larger gains indicate that the program strengthened effort and motivation, while the smaller gains show that language skills and general information — at least as measured by "standard" (i.e., somewhat culture-bound) tests — are more stubbornly rooted in early experience, and so are harder to change by means of a program of the limited strength and duration of ours.

On the other hand, black females in the program — to our surprise — showed no gain in Persistence in School (they were, in fact, fractionally behind their controls). A large proportion were finishing high school with or without a special program, and our stimulus may have been insufficient to push a significantly larger proportion of them over the threshold into college. It should be noted, however, that in the 1964 cohort of black females the experimentals attained much higher levels of Persistence than the controls. As they were the oldest group, their situation is perhaps the most crucial test. Black females were ahead of black males in achievement tests and grades before the program began, so it is not surprising that, compared with their matched partners, they made smaller gains; they had less room for improvement. Nevertheless, in every case changes were in the expected direction.

Nonblack males moved only insignificantly ahead of their control partners in Persistence in School. We have some informal evidence that peer group standards as well as parental values tend to dampen interest in college. Meanwhile, aspiration to college was mounting in black communities. On the other measures the scores of nonblack males exceeded those of their control partners, significantly so in the case of Achievement Tests. Somehow the program improved their performance in secondary school, but did not increase their efforts to get in to college.

Nonblack females are the smallest group. Those in the experimental group, vis-à-vis their partners, made the largest absolute gain on Persistence in School, but the difference was not significant. All the other comparisons were in the expected direction, that on Achievement Tests to a significant degree.

The data presented in Chapter 4 and summarized in Table 5.1 leave little doubt that the Special Opportunity Program made a difference. Our evidence refutes the belief that intellectual and academic development are frozen at an early age and that a child's environment prevents educational intervention from affecting motivation and performance. On the contrary, it shows that the provision of expanded opportunities, the enlargement of the range of cultural experience, the encouragement of skill and the heightening of aspiration, all in a context that promotes continuity of the initial experience, can significantly affect educational outcomes.

We definitely do not say that we have a panacea for educational deprivation. Clearly, in the early years stimulation and nutrition, for example, are vital to later development, as are also the quality of primary-school training, the community resources, the general economic level, and the range of opportunities perceived as available (Coleman, 1971).

It would have been dramatic to discover either that our program made no significant difference between our experimental and control groups, confirming a widespread pessimistic conviction, or that the difference was large, documenting how easily accumulated educational deficits could be overcome. What we did find were results in the ambiguous middle ground. Although it cannot revolutionize the course of development, a brief but energetic program early in secondary school can make an essential contribution. Coming at a time critical in the formation of identity and the sketching of a life plan, for some it can change a vicious circle into an upward spiral.

Candor dictates a caveat: we cannot specify systematically just how much specific activities contributed to the effect our program produced. How instructive it would be to a school if we could report that, for examples, activity A brought three times the benefit to most of our pupils as was brought by activity B; or that offering A and B produced an effect not appreciably increased by adding C; or that, in a pinch, a

Table 5.1. *Multiple Classification Analysis of the net effects of the Special Opportunity Program on five dependent variables* (*summary table*)

Advantage of experimental over control partner	N	Persistence in School	Assignment to Special Track	Achievement Tests	Junior High Grades	Senior High Grades
1. Total group	270	+n.s.	<.01	<.001	<.001	<.01
2. Males	182	+n.s.	<.05	<.001	<.01	<.05
3. Females	88	+n.s.	+.10	<.01	<.10	+n.s.
4. Blacks	186	+n.s.	<.01	<.10	<.01	<.05
5. Non-Blacks	84	+n.s.	+n.s.	<.001	<.10	+n.s.
6. Black males	131	+n.s.	<.10	+n.s.	<.05	<.10
7. Nonblack males	51	+n.s.	+n.s.	<.05	+n.s.	+n.s.
8. Black females	55	−n.s.	<.05	<.10	+n.s.	+n.s.
9. Nonblack females	33	+n.s.	+n.s.	<.05	+n.s.	+n.s.
10. Rows 7, 8, and 9 combined	139	+n.s.	+.05	<.001	<.05	+n.s.

+n.s. = not significant but in hypothesized direction.
−n.s. = not significant and contrary to hypothesized direction.

school should certainly adopt A, then choose between B and C. Such specifications would also aid scholars to develop theories to explain social behavior. But in order to achieve this precision, our original intervention and the data we gathered would have had to be different—a state of affairs of which we have been aware ever since we began to analyze the data. Unfortunately, the intervention program and our budget for analysis did not allow a more refined design: three experimental and control groups, for example. Our data are most complete on the experimental group and the first batch of matched controls. The second control group (similar in initial status, but in schools beyond the influence of our intervention) yielded less complete data, partly because the separation from our intervention made it harder to keep in touch.

We should also call attention to the problem of the so-called Hawthorne Effect. In Chapter 2 we report our efforts to keep our pupils out of the limelight. We did not want their teachers to expect more than was warranted and, too, we sought to protect the pupils from undue attention when teachers discovered their participation in a special program. We believe — partly because most of our pupils were soon dispersed in various high schools where they were lost in big crowds — that we succeeded in these objectives. However, more important to the Hawthorne (or, to refer to later research, to the Pygmalion-in-the-classroom) problem than teachers' perceptions, are the pupils' self-perceptions. Years ago, workers at Hawthorne produced more partly because they felt they were in an experiment. More recently, pupils in the Pygmalion classrooms in California responded to their teachers' expectations by behaving as they realized they were expected to behave. This particular finding, reported by Rosenthal and Jacobson in 1968, called wide attention to the relation between teachers' expectation and pupils' performance. It has been severely criticized as methodologically defective (e.g., for one extended example see J. Jung, 1971). But Rosenthal, the senior author, has stimulated around the world over a hundred related studies of the self-fulfilling prophecy, most of them reinforcing his contention. However the Rosenthal and Jacobson study is viewed, there is ample evidence in over half a century of research to support the hypothesis that encouragement has a stimulating effect. In our program of intervention, encouragement to succeed, even to excel, was inherent. We made conscious efforts to promote high expectations. The summer experience was the most obvious phase, but everything else was chosen for its probable contribution to high aspirations. So, on the one hand, it was important to obviate inappropriate, unthinking, automatic treatment of pupils by publicizing their participation in a special program; but on the other hand, within the program itself, and even in ways not immediately recognized by pupils or families, it was necessary to build morale by emphasizing opportunities, urging responsibility for developing talent, rewarding effort.

We would like to emphasize, in connection with the unintended effects of social research, that most social experiments represent first-stage innovations, with their results affected by "newness" and associated "Hawthorne" processes. Second-stage pilot programs are urgently needed to separate such effects from the specific program features under study but, typically, refinements of this sort are not part of the policy of foundations' public investment. Even major social experiments, such as the New Jersey Negative Income Tax Experiment, suffer from lack of procedures designed to sort out the effects under study from the unintended allied effects. We believe that it is essential that second and third "generation" studies of promising social programs be funded.

A closely related problem is reactive leakage which, by obscuring the difference between experimental and control pupils' experiences, can contaminate effects. We believe we minimized it by the variety of precautions detailed in Chapter 2. If there was significant leakage, it was not between experimentals and controls, but due rather to the great social pressures on all our pupils. As we have mentioned, there has been a major growth of opportunity for all minorities in the United States since we started our program in 1964, but how much it affected our results we cannot tell, because it worked upon experimentals and controls alike. We have no way to test (as some have suggested) whether it made more difference to our experimental pupils because they and their families were becoming increasingly sensitive to upward striving and thus might have been more responsive to national support of minorities. Even were there such an interactive effect, it could not have occurred without the experimental stimuli.

Lessons from the Middle Start program

After seven years of work in the field we sometimes long for the small-group laboratory and the twenty-minute interaction. In a different mood, we long for another seven years in which to repeat the experiment, for we believe that we could avoid many deviations from our ideal design. Thus we would specify more clearly in advance what we expected from the cooperating school systems; we would draw from a smaller range of schools, in order to reduce problems of communication and transportation; we would recognize from the start the importance of the follow-up program.

It is probably inevitable that those who experiment in the field must adjust to the wide variety of persons and situations that influence the interaction under study. We dealt with five school systems, differing in regulations, attitudes, tests, and methods of keeping records. We followed 195 pairs of students through several dynamic years when national and local policies and the attitudes of many disadvantaged families were changing profoundly. We have several sets of data on each child; but on no set is our information complete. Although the rates of return on the original pupil data form, on the continuing record of school performance, on the family interview, and on the mailed questionnaire have, in every instance, been high (never under 80 percent), we have had to estimate some information and to set aside a few comparisons for lack of adequate measurement.

In spite of these difficulties, we believe we can speak with some confidence about various aspects of a Middle Start program. The most impressive lesson to us is the appreciation of the importance of paying attention to each new experience, each new challenge, if a child is going to learn to cope effectively with school. It does little good to give a stimulating and attractive summer program if it is not supported afterward. By themselves, many of our students would not have found out how to take advantage of opportunities in their schools and cities, how to understand the financing of a college education, even how to get college catalogues and admission forms, and how necessary are preparatory courses of study. Without counseling, they would not have been able to put their new motivation into action. It is perhaps too much to say that critical learning situations in the ages from thirteen to eighteen are, as we suggested in Chapter 1, like links in a chain — if one link is broken or missing, the chain will not hold — but the analogy is not far from the truth. We have also learned that the same thing continues after disadvantaged students get into college. Each year, new and often unanticipated problems confront them, for they are moving in a somewhat strange and unfamiliar culture. Any *one* of their experiences can break the continuity, bringing back a sense of defeat, or hostility, or isolation, feelings that can weaken or even crush the desire to continue.

These, then, are the ingredients for success in a Middle Start program:

First, an exciting, new, stretching experience—in our case, taking pupils out of their home communities and bringing them to a college campus—an experience that breaks the connection in their minds between school and failure, school and discrimination, school and boredom. In this first summer they form new friendships, encounter various adult models, and discover more academic, artistic, and recreational activities than they have known before.

Second, a sponsor to show that new possibilities are available, and to explain each step along the way. In our case, the staff and director of the Special Opportunities Program, college-age counselors, and school teachers and counselors served as such sponsors, although not with as much continuing support as was actually needed. Neither our budget nor our level of experience was sufficient to carry out this part of the program as we would have liked.

Third, a circle of "supporting others." Although less likely to perform the instrumental tasks carried out by the sponsors, these serve to give emotional support, to recognize and encourage the changes in a pupil's motivation, and, as college age approaches, to help financially, if only in a small way. Parents are the most important members of the circle, but other relatives, family friends, and adults in the community are also significant. Because this kind of support is essential, a program that deals with pupils only will have a high rate of failure. By means of reunions involving the families, by newsletters, and by interviews (which, although designed as a source of information, proved often to be a source of encouragement), we sought to identify and strengthen the concern of the supporters. Parents were often extraordinarily cooperative. Reunions were well attended; some families demonstrated their interest by driving hundreds of miles to attend them, at a cost they could ill afford. The testimonials we received document not simply appreciation of the program, but the strong motivation of most parents to encourage their children in maximum educational effort, once they realize that a path has been opened.

Each of the three ingredients is essential. When they are present in a significant proportion of children from disadvantaged backgrounds, skills, motivation, and academic performance can be raised. Our participants and our controls, it should be remembered, were drawn from disadvantaged families, but they were visible in their schools as children of some promise. Indicators pointed to them, not as strong pupils al-

ready destined for success, but as promising subjects who, with sufficient support, could move ahead. Their course grades or achievement
test scores were better than average, or their teachers saw them, despite
poor grades and test scores, as persons with unused talent. We are un-
able to say that students who are not identified by any one of these
indicators could be helped by the procedures we have described. It is
our judgment, however, based on the performance of many pupils of
high risk, that there is a great deal of hidden potential among disadvantaged children, that carefully planned programs with *continuous* support
through a number of years can be of great value to many in junior high
school who seem, by available measures, to be headed for failure.

Our total program cost less than $2,000 per child over a five-year
period for each cohort. We did not set up a strong follow-up program
until a year after we had started, and staff changes weakened it in the
last months. We did not have funds to bring the pupils back to campus
for a second summer, probably at the end of their sophomore year in
high school. Despite these limitations, one quarter of our participants
showed significantly greater improvement — as measured by the combined set of dependent variables — than their matched partners.

On a budget of $3,000 per child ($1,000 more than we had, yet
barely the cost of one year in prep school for many persons in the
upper and upper-middle classes), we are confident that half or more of
the participants in a program similar to but stronger than ours, would
improve significantly in academic motivation and performance, compared to matched controls. Total costs to society over a lifetime would
be negligible. Indeed, the investment would doubtless be returned many
times.

Unexpected additional consequences

Our description of the effects of the program would be incomplete if
we failed to mention several indirect consequences on persons other
than the students themselves. We can only call attention to these additional influences because we cannot document them with precision.
Nevertheless, a flood of impressions, based on conversations, direct observation, unsolicited testimonials, and other evidence, convince us that
our summer and follow-up programs have significantly influenced a
wide circle of persons.

Among our most active and important participants were the college-age counselors. They lived in the dormitories with the Middle Starters, helped them with their work, showed them how to deal with new and sometimes confusing circumstances of life away from home, joined them in recreation, welcomed them at reunions, and sometimes visited them in their high schools after their summer on the campus. We have no doubt that the college counselors were an important ingredient in the program. But what we are emphasizing here is that they learned more than they taught. Almost all wanted to return for another summer; their interest in race relations, in problems of the city, in education, was strengthened. Many of them, in particular the black counselors, grew in ability to see a difficulty not solely as a personal problem but as a public issue, to be dealt with only by understanding its structural sources.

The program was scarcely less important for the participating teachers who, though selected on the basis of their interest and skill in programs of supportive education, had in few cases been directly involved in such programs as ours. They remarked that their teaching had changed; their sensitivity to the concerns of students and their interest in academic policy had grown.

Our evidence of the effect on our participants' families is not direct, but from our interviews and conversations at reunions we see that parents and siblings, older as well as younger, have been drawn into the program's sphere of influence. We feared some negative effects — alienation of a child from his family, antagonism of parents, jealousy of a brother or sister — and undoubtedly this has sometimes occurred; but our techniques have not been sensitive enough to detect such instances and we are confident that the positive effects are much the stronger.

The sacrifices made by families of children to attend reunions at the college, some coming from long distances, are evidence of their interest in sharing the informational and recreational events. They raised money by bake sales and other projects to send members — the children and their parents or guardians — to the campus; some took all-night bus rides; some three-generation households came from nearby by whatever means were available. The impact on parents can also be seen in the activities they undertook to help their children and other children in the community who had been in the special program. One mother, after being instructed with her child in how to fill out complicated college admissions forms and the parent's confidential financial statement, became virtually a local admissions counselor. Early in the fall she systematically called on parents with graduating children, to make sure that both children and parents had sent for and received the needed forms, filled them out on schedule, obtained fee-waiver forms where needed, and kept in contact with the schools and the SOP staff as required. In each school district several parents took the lead in maintaining a steady stream of information about college and in organizing related school and parental activities.

Several of our interviewers became strongly interested in continuing actively to assist disadvantaged children. Working closely with both experimental and control groups of parents and guardians, they began to realize the need of programs to support college-bound pupils. (Although interviewers were not told which families had the experimental children and which had the controls, the information usually came out by the end of an interview.) Almost immediately, one interviewer went to work for a large city school district in a program to encourage disadvantaged but talented children to go to college; a second interviewer accepted employment in community liaison work of the same sort, in another large city school district.

More indirect, but worthy of mention, are the consequences on the participating institutions. In the course of a seven-year program, hundreds of school and college officials and teachers heard about "special opportunities," discussed them, and helped in the making of decisions. The minds and interests of a score of Oberlin College professors and administrators were stretched; on campus, work with undergraduates from disadvantaged backgrounds improved, partly because of lessons learned in the summer program. Administrators and teachers in the school systems from which our participants came have raised new questions about their own procedures and aims, as their support of the Special Opportunity Program helped them to see the range of problems in their schools and to support other activities.

We do not know how to add up these indirect effects; in the light of our values, we may be inclined to exaggerate them. But we have seen signs of them all around us. We have not seen signs of indirect negative effects. In the long run, such a program as we have described may prove to be a middle start for all who have been involved, and not alone for those whom, in an imprecise way, we have called the "participants."

Appendix A. Suggestions for selection procedures for summer
Special Educational Opportunity Program

A memorandum to participating schools

Aims of selection

A major goal in the suggestions listed below for selecting seventh and
eighth graders for the summer enrichment program at Oberlin College
is to recruit students with high potential and ability for work in higher
education. The program is experimental in the sense that we need to
know which type of student will benefit, and in what ways, from the
planned program of instruction and cocurricular activities. Thus, the
hope is to recruit both "low-risk high achievers" who show up in many
ways as able students and some "high-risk high achievers" who show up
in some ways as talented students. Listed below are selection procedures and the criteria on which they will be based. In addition, suggested proportions of "low-risk/high-promise" students and "high-risk/high-
promise students" are described.

Criteria. Three sets of criteria are important in selecting students for
this program: (1) Criteria that define eligibility among students from
"severely disadvantaged backgrounds"; (2) Criteria that define "promising talent," both as to risk and promise for higher education; and (3)
Criteria that define "behavioral problems" that may be critical for the
success and effectiveness of this program.

   1. *Severely disadvantaged background.* Three criteria *jointly* define
      the eligibility of students for this program:
         (a) Limited financial resources. To be eligible, the student
             comes from a family with limited financial resources. A
             student may be considered eligible if his family would have
             to cut down the purchase of basic necessities (clothing,
             food, shelter) in order to help finance his future education.
         (b) Limited neighborhood opportunities. The student also
             lives in an area where neighborhood resources for encour-

110

aging and stimulating higher educational plans and aspirations are relatively undeveloped.

    (c) Minority status. Because of race, ethnicity, or regional background, the students are not likely to receive the same opportunities for higher education as those who are not subject to discrimination.

2. *Promising talent.* Among seventh and eighth graders from given schools in these neighborhoods, the following criteria are proposed for selection of students on the basis of promise or talent and risk. We can consider all students who show up well in one or more of these criteria as promising or talented. On the other hand, we feel (whether correctly or not) that there is less risk with some students and more with others among the talented. One way of identifying the risk involved in aiding a given student is on the basis of whether he shows up well in all the criteria of selection for talent or whether he shows up with only some positive signs. Those who show up with many positive signs would be considered "low risk" compared with those who show up with only one positive sign (teacher nominations, for example) among all potential criteria.

    Four sources of talent are recommended to select the students:

    (a) Information from a test(s) of intelligence

    (b) Information from achievement tests

    (c) Information from grades in school

    (d) Information from teacher nominations

The "cutting points" for each selection criterion will have to be worked out with each school system because different test measures are employed among the participating groups. If the "normal" cutting points for identifying good risks for higher education are established for the schools, the high-promise students would represent those who are above the cutting point, the low-promise students would be those below it. It should be noted that for each of the selection criteria, all of the students in the given grades may or may not be of high promise. They may be of high promise in some criteria but of low promise in others. What is desired here is as large a "talent pool" by available criteria as possible to give these students a chance to participate in the summer program.

   (a) Intelligence test scores. If the normal cutting point is 130 points, the lower limit would be at 110 points and above. The general rule would be to include in this listing those students who are about 20 percent below the normal cutting point for selection into a college preparatory program.

   (b) Achievement tests. The lower limit would be one grade score below the given grade in which the student is found (in academic—college prep work).

   (c) Grades. The lower limit would be one grade below the given grade (averaged) considered necessary for counseling students to follow through for college work in academic—college prep subjects.

   (d) Teacher nominations. The procedure to follow would be to suggest any other students who would not be high-promise students by test or grade scores as well as those who are high achievement by other criteria. This is to insure that as large a number as possible of talented students by any of these four measures (a—d) will appear on the eligible list.

3. *Behavioral problems.* Criteria defining these should be used to aid in the selection of students for the summer program so that a *wide* range of talented students can be included. The intent here is to note any *serious* problems which students might bring to the residential experience that might be detrimental to themselves and to other students in the program. The aim is not to exclude the students with behavior problems, but to include those who appear to be talented and who could benefit from this program.

This summer program, as structured now, cannot adequately service the talented students who have *severe* behavioral problems in the schools and the community. These students may require more support and assistance than this program can provide. The point to note is that where school officials (teachers, counselors, and principals included) can provide information on students as to severity of behavioral problems, the staff of this program can preplan for these students. We would like to see a few students (up to 10 percent) who are of high promise but have some behavioral problems in order to aid them where possible.

Procedure: The following is a set of suggestions for achieving a fair selection of students from different talent—risk groupings in relation to the goals of the experimental program at Oberlin.

1. Develop a list of nominees in each of the four criteria of talent in terms of high achievers (or those above the selected cutting point) and low achievers (or those below the cutting point).

    (a) Begin with the list of students on the basis of intelligence tests.

    (b) Next, develop a list of students on the basis of achievement tests.

    (c) Next, develop a list of students on the basis of grades. From this list, exclude all students below the cutting point (high-risk students) in grades, *if* they do not show up as promising in intelligence or achievement scores.

    (d) Finally, develop a list of promising students with nominations from teachers in the seventh and eighth grades. This list should contain those names of students *who do not show up in any of the criteria above* as well as those who are of "known promise" by one or more of the first criteria.

    (e) Separate the boys' list from that of the girls.

2. Classify each student into one of two "promise risk" groups below.

    (a) Students who show up as high-promise students in *all four* of the talent criteria above should be placed in the high achievers group.

    (b) If the size of the group which is of high promise in all four criteria is small, place the students who are of high promise in at least three of the four criteria in the high achievers group. If not, place them in the low achievers group below.

    (c) Place the students who are high achieving in only two or one of the four criteria of talent into the low achievers' group.

3. Aim to get a large proportion of high achievers (80 percent) and a lesser proportion of low achievers (20 percent).

    (a) Rate each student at to severity of behavior problems for the summer program. Exclude those students who require a level of supervision that cannot be provided by the program.

(b) Sample within the high achievers group until the number of students desired is obtained (80 percent of the total number of students coming to the summer program from the schools).

(c) Sample within the low achievers group until the number of students (20 percent of the total number of students invited from the schools) is obtained.

(d) Go over the list to see if the percentage of students with somewhat severe behavior problems represents no more than 10 percent of the total number of students. Among this 10 percent the hope is to obtain students who are "natural leaders," and who may be somewhat difficult to handle but are of high potential.

Appendix B. Persistence and attainment: Observations from
a partial sample[1]

We noted in Chapter 4 that our Persistence in School variable was not
well measured because the 1965 and 1966 cohorts were still of high
school age at the time of our last full-scale inquiry. Significant differentiation between experimental and control group is not likely to show
up until after high school graduation. Fortunately we have some data
from 1973, secured in a mailed questionnaire sent out by Professor
Donald Campbell and his staff (to whom we express our sincere thanks),
that permit some reasonable conjecture, if not precise statement, about
the extent of persistence in school among our respondents. Because the
rate of return was quite low (25 percent), we offer here what we think
to be reasonable interpretations, but they cannot be regarded as firm
conclusions. By commenting on the 1973 data in the context of some
observations about the evidence from 1970, we can note probable
trends.

High school attainment

In April 1970, we found that the 1965 and 1966 cohorts, both experimental and control, were on schedule in their high school programs (Table B.1). (Only the 1964 group was of college age.) Some members of
the staffs of the schools with which we worked had expected the program to alienate the children from regular school work — in reaction
against its routines compared with the excitement of the summer's experience — but no such effect is discernible. Participants in the program
were slightly farther along in their high school courses than their control partners.

We also secured a statement of intention from the 1965 and 1966 cohorts. Members of the experimental group were significantly more likely (p = <.01) to indicate their intention to enroll in a four-year college
or university than those in the control group. This is a fairly weak finding, to be sure, because the experimentals' rate of positive responses

115

Table B.1. *Educational status of the 1965 and 1966 cohorts, as of April 1970 (in percent)*

Educational status	Experi-mental	Control	Total
1965			
Expected to graduate from high school, June	84	79	81
Still in 11th grade or below or unknown[a]	16	21	19
Total	100	100	100
N	(70)	(70)	(140)
1966			
Expected to graduate from high school, June	16	15	15
Expected to enter 12th grade in September	81	75	78
In 11th grade or below or unknown[b]	3	10	7
Total	100	100	100
N	(69)	(69)	(138)

[a] 1 experimental, 5 controls with missing data.
[b] 2 experimentals and 7 controls with missing data.

may in part be a function of having received an inquiry from the college that had sponsored a valued summer program.

Four-year college attainment

If we look at one aspect of the Persistence in School variable — the likelihood of attending a four-year college or university — we find that the incomplete 1973 data set presents very much the same picture as the quite complete 1970 data set, giving us some confidence that, despite the low rate of return in 1973, we have a valid measure. As a major aim of the program was to increase rates of attendance at four-year colleges, these findings are worthy of note.

Various comparisons are found in Table B.2. Whether one looks at the 1970 or the 1973 figures (lines 1 and 2), one finds a ratio of about 1½ : 1 in the experimental–control rates of college attendance. (The 1970 rates are low, of course, because two of the cohorts are still in high school.) Neither difference is significant, although the 1973 comparison falls just short of the .10 level, despite the small sample. When only the 1964 cohort is compared (lines 3 and 4), the differences are significant at the .05 level for both the 1970 and the 1973 sets of data. It is also interesting to observe that our black participants, using the 1970 data for the 1964 group, are significantly ($p = <.05$) more likely

Table B.2. *Persistence in school as measured by attendance at a four-year institution*

Cohort	N	% ever attended 4-year institution	Mean	Standard deviation	Standard error	Variation	Two-tailed probability[a]
1. Total, 1970							
Experimental	189	14.0	2.810	1.812	.132	3.283	+n.s.
Control	182	9.0	2.610	1.522	.113	2.317	
2. Total, 1973							
Experimental	53	53.0	5.264	1.534	.211	2.353	+n.s.
Control	44	36.0	4.795	1.440	.220	2.073	
3. 1964 group, 1970							
Experimental	53	48.0	4.698	1.907	.262	3.638	<.05
Control	55	28.0	3.873	1.599	.216	2.558	
4. 1964 group, 1973							
Experimental	15	73.0	5.900	1.242	.321	1.542	<.05
Control	14	43.0	4.710	1.297	.342	1.682	
5. 1964 black cohort, 1970							
Experimental	35	50.0	4.829	2.093	.359	2.593	<.05
Control	33	30.0	4.030	1.610	.283	2.303	
6. 1965–66 cohorts, 1973							
Experimental	38	45.0	4.974	1.525	.209	2.326	+n.s.
Control	30	34.0	4.767	1.524	.225	2.323	

[a] (+) = advantage to the experimental group.

Table B.3. *Educational attainments among 1965 and 1966 pupils by 1973 (in percent)*

Type of attainment	Experi-mental	Control	Total
Select four-year college	21	17	19
Four-year college	24	17	21
Junior College or post-high school technical schools[a]	21	30	25
High school graduation[b]	34	36	35
Total	100	100	100
N	(38)	(30)	(68)

[a] One child reported technical school placement.
[b] No reports of noncompletion of high school studies.

to be attending a four-year college or university than their control partners (line 5). When we combine the 1965 and 1966 groups, using the 1973 data (line 6), the difference is not significant, although it is in the hypothesized direction.

Assuming this to be a valid comparison, we are uncertain about the reasons for the difference between the 1964 and the 1965–66 groups. One interpretation is that the 1964 children, being our first selections, were somehow different from those in the 1965 and 1966 groups. The two later groups may have contained higher proportions of children with lower levels of community and family support. Another interpretation is that the burgeoning of junior colleges and two-year college branches in and near our research communities encouraged more children to go beyond high school. When this is coupled with increased attention to equal educational opportunities for minority children, the effects of the experimental program may have been masked. We might also note that there were "John Henry effects" — compensatory placement by school staffs of children who had been nominated for our program but not selected in our random assignment (Campbell, 1975). Finally, the full effects of the program on persistence had not yet, in 1973, had time to be demonstrated for the 1965 and 1966 groups. Those "on schedule" would have been sophomores or juniors in college. Some in two-year colleges have transferred or will transfer to four-year programs.

In spite of these possible influences, the 1965 and 1966 groups were, judging from the 1973 replies, more likely to be attending four-year colleges (Table B.3), although not at a significantly higher rate.

Notes

Chapter 1. The sources of academic achievement

1 See, for example, William H. Sewell, 1971. "Inequality of Opportunity for Higher Education," *American Sociological Review* 36: 793—809; Richard A. Rehberg, Walter E. Schafer, and Judie Sinclair, 1970. "Toward a Temporal Sequence of Adolescent Achievement Variables," *American Sociological Review* 35: 34—48; Robert B. Smith, 1972. "Neighborhood Context and College Plans: An Ordinal Path Analysis," *Social Forces* 51: 199—217; Allan Svensson, 1971. *Relative Achievement: School Performance in Relation to Intelligence, Sex and Home Environment*, Almquist and Wiksell; Christopher Jencks *et al.*, 1972. *Inequality: A Reassessment of the Effect of Family and Schooling in America*, Basic Books; Chad Gordon, 1973. *Looking Ahead*, American Sociological Association; Robert M. Hauser, 1972. *Socioeconomic Background and Educational Performance*, American Sociological Association.

2 James S. Coleman *et al.*, 1966. *Equality of Educational Opportunity*, U.S. Government Printing Office; Robert L. Crain and Carol Sachs Weisman, 1972. *Discrimination, Personality, Achievement: A Survey of Northern Blacks*, Seminar Press; Nancy St. John and Ralph Lewis, 1971. "The Influence of School Racial Context on Academic Achievement," *Social Problems* 19: 68—79; S. O. Roberts and Carell P. Horton, 1973. "Extent of and Effects of Desegregation," chap. 10 in Kent S. Miller and Ralph M. Dreger (eds.), *Comparative Studies of Blacks and Whites in the United States*, Seminar Press; Alan B. Wilson, 1969. *The Consequences of Segregation: Academic Achievement in a Northern Community*, Glendessary Press.

3 Julian C. Stanley (ed.), 1973. *Compensatory Education for Children, Ages 2—8*, Johns Hopkins University Press; Nathan W. Gottfried, 1973. "Effects of Early Intervention Programs," chap. 9 in Kent S. Miller and Ralph M. Dreger (eds.), *Comparative Studies of Blacks and Whites in the United States*, Seminar Press; J. McV. Hunt, 1969. "Has Compensatory Education Failed? Has It Been Attempted?" *Harvard Educational Review* 39: 278—300; Edmund W. Gordon and Doxey A. Wilkerson, 1966. *Compensatory Education for the Disadvantaged: Programs and Practices Preschool Through College*, College Entrance Examination Board; David E. Hunt and Robert H. Hardt, 1966. "The Effect of Upward Bound Programs on the Attitudes, Motivation and Academic Achievement of Negro Students," *Journal of Social Issues* 25: 117—29; Edmund W. Gordon, 1970. "Compensatory Education: Evaluation in Perspective," *IRCD Bulletin* 6.

4 See, for example, Robert Ardrey, 1966. *Territorial Imperative*, Atheneum; Konrad Lorenz, 1960. *On Aggression*, Harcourt Brace Jovanovich. For valuable commentary on this thesis, see Ashley Montagu (ed.), 1972. *Man and Aggression*, 2nd edn, Oxford University Press; Pierre L. van den Berghe, 1974. "Bringing Beasts Back In: Toward a Biosocial Theory of Aggression," *American Sociological Review* 39: 777—88.

5 Arthur R. Jensen, 1969. "How Much Can We Boost IQ and Scholastic Achievement?" *Harvard Educational Review* 39: 1—123; Audrey M. Shuey, 1966. *The Testing of Negro Intelligence*, 2nd edn, Social Science Press; R. J. Herrnstein, 1971. "I.Q.," *The Atlantic* 288: 43—64. For critiques of this point of view, see Margaret Mead, Theodosius Dobzhansky, Ethel Tobach, and Robert Light (eds.), 1968. *Science and the Concept of Race*, Columbia University Press.

6 Esther P. Edwards, 1968. "Kindergarten is Too Late," *Saturday Review* 45 (June 15): 68 ff. For more analytic and less pessimistic examinations of this question, see the chapters by J. M. Hunt, Carl Bereiter, and Celia B. Stendler-Lavatelli, chaps. 8, 9, 10 in Martin Deutsch, Irwin Katz, and Arthur R. Jensen (eds.), 1968. *Social Class, Race and Psychological Development*, Holt, Rinehart and Winston.

7 On the culture of poverty see, for example, Oscar Lewis, 1959. *Five Families: Mexican Case Studies in the Culture of Poverty*, Basic Books; Oscar Lewis, 1961. *The Children of Sanchez*, Random House; Oscar Lewis, 1966. *La Vida: A Puerto Rican Family in the Culture of Poverty*, Random House; Edward Banfield, 1958. *The Moral Basis of a Backward Society*, Free Press; Edward Banfield, 1968. *The Unheavenly City: The Nature and Future of Our Urban Crisis*, Little, Brown; Michael Harrington, 1962. *The Other America: Poverty in the United States*, Macmillan; Herbert Gans, 1962. *The Urban Villagers*, Macmillan; Walter B. Miller, 1958. "Lower Class Culture as a Generating Milieu of Gang Delinquency," *Journal of Social Issues* 14: 5—19. For critiques, see Charles Valentine, 1968. *Culture and Poverty*, University of Chicago Press; Jack Roach and Orville Gursslin, 1967. "An Evaluation of the Concept 'Culture of Poverty,'" *Social Forces* 45: 383—92; Seymour Parker and Robert J. Kleiner, 1970. "The Culture of Poverty: An Adjustive Dimension," *American Anthropologist* 72: 516—27; Lee Rainwater, 1970. "The Problem of Lower Class Culture," *Journal of Social Issues* 26: 133—48; George E. Simpson and J. Milton Yinger, 1972. *Racial and Cultural Minorities*, 4th edn, Harper & Row, 172—7; Theodore D. Graves, 1974. "Urban Indian Personality and the 'Culture of Poverty,'" *American Ethnologist* 1: 65—86; L. Richard Della Fave, 1974. "The Culture of Poverty Revisited: A Strategy for Research," *Social Problems* 21: 609—21; Barbara Coward, J. Allen Williams, Jr., and Joe R. Feagin, 1974. "The Culture of Poverty Debate: Some Additional Data," *Social Problems* 21: 621—34; Elliot Liebow, 1967. *Tally's Corner: A Study of Negro Streetcorner Men*, Little, Brown.

8 See, for example, James S. Coleman *et al.*, 1966. *Equality of Educational Opportunity*, U.S. Government Printing Office; David Hargreaves, 1967. *Social Relations in a Secondary School*, Humanities Press; Robert Rosenthal and Lenore Jacobson, 1968. *Pygmalion in the Classroom*, Holt, Rinehart and Winston. For basic studies dealing with many variables that influence achievement, see O. D. Duncan, D. L. Featherman, and Beverly Duncan, 1972. *Socioeconomic Background and Achievement*, Seminar Press; and Raymond Boudon, 1973. *Education, Opportunity and Social Inequality: Changing Prospects in Western Society*, Wiley.

9 On the gap between aspirations and expectations, see, for example, Wan Sang Han, 1969. "Two Conflicting Themes: Common Values Versus Class Differential Values," *American Sociological Review* 34: 679—90; R. N. Stephenson, 1957. "Mobility Orientation and Stratification of 1,000 Ninth Graders," *American Sociological Review* 22: 204—12; Hyman Rodman, 1963. "The Lower Class Value Stretch," *Social Forces* 42: 205—15.

10 As the geneticist, Hirsch (1970) has said in reaction to Jensen's recent conclusion that inherited factors account for the bulk of intelligence differences, a heritability estimate is a piece of knowledge that is "both deceptive and trivial." "High or low heritability tell us absolutely nothing about how a given individual might have developed under conditions different from those in which he actually did develop." *The Times Educational Supplement* (July 24): 9. For a brilliant interpretation of the interaction of nature and nurture, see Theodosius Dobzhansky, 1973. *Genetic Diversity and Human Equality*, Basic Books.

11 For an attempt to formulate such a theory, see J. Milton Yinger, 1965. *Toward a Field Theory of Behavior*, McGraw-Hill. On the concept of "interaction," see John Atkinson, 1957. "Motivational Determinants of Risk-Taking Behavior," *Psychological Review* 64: 359—72; Hubert Blalock, Jr., 1965. "Theory Building and the Statistical Concept of Interaction," *American Sociological Review* 30: 374—80; and Bruce Eckland, 1967. "Genetics and Sociology: A Reconsideration," *American Sociological Review* 32: 173—94. For

empirical studies that emphasize multivariate analysis of educational behavior, sometimes with an additive model, sometimes with a product model, see Ralph H. Turner, 1964. *The Social Context of Ambition*, Chandler; William Sewell, Archibald Haller and Alejandro Portes, 1969. "The Educational and Early Occupational Attainment Process," *American Sociological Review* 34: 82–92; Chad Gordon, 1973. *Looking Ahead*, American Sociological Association: James N. Porter, 1974. "Race, Socialization and Mobility in Educational and Early Occupational Attainment," *American Sociological Review* 39: 303–16.

12 Cf. the systematic efforts to measure and evaluate the effects of different variables upon school-test performance (student attitudes, characteristics of the peer groups, environmental characteristics, teacher quality, and school resources) in the Equality of Opportunity report. Coleman's effort to partition the weights from selected variables and to determine main effects and joint effects (in a nonregression analysis sense) is a search for order in these data. See James S. Coleman, 1970. "Reply to Cain and Watts," *American Sociological Review* 35: 242–52. Also Glen G. Cain and Harold W. Watts, 1970. "Problems in Making Policy Inferences from the Coleman Report," *American Sociological Review* 35: 228–41; Dennis J. Aigner, 1970. "A Comment on Problems in Making Inferences from the Coleman Report," *American Sociological Review* 35: 249–52.

13 This statement of the problem collapses the four-variable model into a two-variable model. In empirical studies, it is extremely difficult to separate cultural from structural influences, and inherited from learned tendencies. We generally use a two-variable model.

14 Ralph H. Turner, 1964. *The Social Context of Ambition*, Chandler: 207–10. Also Robert A. Ellis and W. Clayton Lane, 1967. "Social Mobility and Social Isolation: A Test of Sorokin's Dissociative Hypothesis," *American Sociological Review* 32: 237–46, on the effects of recruiting students for college from different social strata and ethnic–racial backgrounds on both the students and the institutions involved.

15 Marshall S. Smith and Joan S. Bissell, 1970. "Report Analysis: The Impact of Head Start," *Harvard Educational Review* 40: 51–104. The whole issue of the *Harvard Educational Review* (1970) deals with evaluations of compensatory education programs, derived from V. Cicirelli, 1969. *The Impact of Head Start: An Evaluation of the Effects of Head Start on Children's Cognitive and Affective Development*, Westinghouse Learning Corporation.

Chapter 2. Methods of the Middle Start program

1 Although three of the authors were members of the committee that sponsored these summer programs, we were not directly involved in their administration. The Rockefeller grant did not include provisions for research; but as members of the committee, we were able to participate in decisions that had research implications, as, for example, the decision to work with junior high school pupils. Fortunately, support from the United States Office of Education allowed us to undertake full-scale research. Thus we carried through parallel activities under separate auspices — an educational program and a field experiment. Undoubtedly there are problems associated with the holding of dual roles; but we believe that our association with the action program added richness to the research. For a discussion of some of the policy questions raised by this kind of research, see Kiyoshi Ikeda, Frank Laycock, and J. Milton Yinger, 1972. "A Seven-Year Program to Prepare Talented Youths for College," *The Urban Review* 5: 41–5.

2 See Welty's technical treatment of ways to interpret program changes in experimental design. This statistical analysis evaluates the differential effects of changes during the course of a program, especially when the changes are in a known direction: Gordon A. Welty, 1969. "The Logic of Evaluation," Educational Resources Institute offprint, Washington: 7–10, 14–15.

3 To suggest the range of material: Erving Goffman, 1963. *Stigma: Notes on the Management of Spoiled Identity*, Prentice-Hall; Walter R. Gove, 1970. "Societal Reaction as an Explanation of Mental Illness: An Evaluation," *American Sociological Review* 35: 873–84; John Hagan, 1973. "Labelling and Deviance: A Case Study in the Sociology of the Interesting," *Social Problems* 20: 447–58; Edwin Lemert, 1972. *Human Deviance*, 2nd edn, Prentice-Hall; Jane R. Mercer, 1971. *Labelling the Mentally Retarded*, University of California Press; Robert Rosenthal and Lenore Jacobson, 1968. *Pygmalion in the Classroom*, Holt, Rinehart, and Winston; Thomas Scheff, 1974. "The Labelling Theory of Mental Illness," *American Sociological Review* 39: 444–52; Paul G. Schervish, 1973. "The Labeling Perspective: Its Bias and Potential in the Study of Political Deviance," *American Sociologist* 8: 47–57; Edwin M. Schur, 1971. *Labeling Deviant Behavior*, Harper & Row; Ralph H. Turner, 1972. "Deviance Avowal as Neutralization of Commitment," *Social Problems* 19: 308–21.

4 See Appendix A for a detailed statement of directions for the selection procedures given to the schools involved.

5 We have substantial data from a second control group (C-2) that we shall use in future analysis. These are materials on pupils in Cleveland schools that we matched with the schools from which Ex and C-1 pupils were drawn. Because the C-2 individuals were not assigned at random, comparison of their educational performance with that of program participants is less powerful than if it were with C-1 individuals. It can, however, help to measure the extent of leakage.

6 We have now available in the literature ready means for systematic evaluation of the power of alternative designs in controlling plausible rival hypotheses to the research hypothesis. The terminology, labeling, and numbering of alternative designs and the listing of the sources of invalidity are fully developed by Donald T. Campbell and Julian L. Stanley, 1963. "Experimental and Quasi-Experimental Designs for Research on Teaching," pp. 171–246 in Nathan L. Gage (ed.), *Handbook of Research in Teaching*, Rand McNally. Campbell and Stanley's discussion also provides guides to the problem of identifying organizational and extra-organizational constraints and encouragements to given arrangements and design procedures. See also Donald T. Campbell, 1969. "Reforms as Experiments," *American Psychologist* 24: 409–29.

7 The use of squared multiple correlations to estimate the communalities is considered a conservative estimate because the squared multiple correlations mathematically represent the least lower bounds of the actual communalities.

8 See Harry H. Harmon, 1967. *Modern Factor Analysis*, University of Chicago Press, for an explanation of the eigenvalue criterion. For a brief but excellent discussion of the premises, methods, and terminology of factor analysis, see R. J. Rummel, 1967. "Understanding Factor Analysis, " *Journal of Conflict Resolution* 11: 444–80.

9 In the extensive literature on problems of validity and reliability in the use of grades, tests, and records of school track, see e.g., Orville G. Brim, Jr. 1969. *American Beliefs and Attitudes About Intelligence*, Russell Sage, especially chap. 5 on accuracy of tests, and chaps. 9 and 10 on ability grouping and reporting of results; Orville G. Brim, Jr., 1965. "American Attitudes Toward Intelligence Tests," *American Psychologist*, 20: 125–30; David A. Goslin, 1963. *The Search for Ability*, Russell Sage, especially chap. 6 ("What Ability Tests Measure"); Leona E. Tyler, 1965. *The Psychology of Human Differences*, 3rd edn, Appleton-Century-Crofts; Philip E. Vernon, 1969. *Intelligence and Cultural Environment*, Methuen; and Ronald J. Samuda, 1973. "Racial Discrimination Through Mental Testing: A Social Critic's Point of View," *IRCD Bulletin*, May.

Chapter 4. Testing a hypothesis by matched pairs

1 Yinger, Ikeda, and Laycock, 1967. "Treating Matching as a Variable in a Sociological Experiment," *American Sociological Review* 32: 801–12; Robert P. Althauser and Donald

Rubin, 1970. "The Computerized Construction of a Matched Sample," *American Journal of Sociology* 76: 325–46. The discussion of matching and randomization in Ernest Greenwood, 1945. *Experimental Sociology, A Study in Method*, Crown Press, is still useful, as is the treatment by F. Stuart Chapin, 1955. *Experimental Design in Sociological Research*, rev. edn, Harper & Row. A classic statement of the use of randomization is found in R.A. Fisher, 1937. *The Design of Experiments*, 2nd edn, Oliver and Boyd. For brief treatments of matching, see, for example, A.L. Edwards, 1950. *Experimental Design in Psychological Research*, Rinehart, chap. 14; Matilda Riley, 1963. *Sociological Research*, Harcourt Brace Jovanovich, 614–20, 635–7; Claire Selltiz, Marie Jahoda, Morton Deutsch, and Stuart W. Cook, 1959. *Research Methods in Social Relations*, rev. edn, Holt, Rinehart and Winston, 98–9, 102–8, and 138–9. One of the best empirical works using matching is the survey of Ronald Freedman and Amos Hawley, 1949. "Unemployment and Migration in the Depression (1930–1935)," *Journal of the American Statistical Association* 44: 260–72. For a recent matching study, see Ralph Schwitzgebel, 1964. *Streetcorner Research*, Harvard University Press.

2 Coefficients of contiguity obtained with inclusion of missing values are very close to those reported for the four clusters in Table 4.1: Cluster 1, .958; Cluster 2, .952; Cluster 3, .977; Cluster 4, .984. This gives additional evidence of the existence of the structure of the distribution of the missing values.

3 In Tables 4.15–4.20, black males appear twice for purposes of different comparisons, but were counted only once in summary statements.

Chapter 5. Toward educational enrichment

1 We shall explore, in later analyses, the effects of varying levels of family support in the context of theory dealing with significant others. In particular, we shall examine the interaction of support from others, individual capabilities, and the program.

Appendix B. Persistence and attainment

1 This follow-up analysis has been supported by the National Science Foundation Grant SOC-7103704-03, Donald T. Campbell, Northwestern University.

References

Aigner, Dennis J. 1970. "A Comment on Problems in Making Inferences from the Coleman Report." *American Sociological Review* 35: 249—52.

Althauser, Ralph P. and Donald Rubin, 1970. "The Computerized Construction of a Matched Sample." *American Journal of Sociology* 76: 325—46.

Andrews, Frank, James Morgan and John Sonquist, 1967. *Multiple Classification Analysis*. Ann Arbor: Institute for Social Research.

Ardrey, Robert, 1966. *Territorial Imperative*. New York: Atheneum.

Astin, Alexander, 1971. *Predicting Academic Performance in College*. New York: Free Press.

Astin, Helen S. 1972. *Higher Education and the Disadvantaged Student*. Washington: Human Services Press.

Atkinson, John, 1957. "Motivational Determinants of Risk-Taking Behavior." *Psychological Review* 64: 359—72.

Ball, Richard, 1968. "A Poverty Case: The Analgesic Subculture of the Southern Appalachians." *American Sociological Review* 33: 885—95.

Banfield, Edward, 1958. *The Moral Basis of a Backward Society*. New York: Free Press.

1968. *The Unheavenly City: The Nature and Future of our Urban Crisis* (rev. edn, 1974). Boston: Little, Brown.

Blalock, Hubert M., Jr., 1965. "Theory Building and the Statistical Concept of Interaction." *American Sociological Review* 30: 374—80.

1970. "Estimating Measurement Error Using Multiple Indicators and Several Points in Time." *American Sociological Review* 35: 101—11.

Blos, Peter, 1971. "The Child Analyst Looks at Young Adolescence."*Daedalus* 100: 961—78.

Boudon, Raymond, 1973. *Education, Opportunity, and Social Inequality: Changing Prospects in Western Society*. New York: Wiley.

Brewer, Marilyn B., Donald T. Campbell and William D..Crano, 1970. "Testing a Single Factor Model as an Alternative to the Misuse of Partial Correlations in Hypothesis-Testing Research," *Sociometry* 33: 1—11.

Brim, Orville G., Jr., 1965. "American Attitudes Toward Intelligence Tests." *American Psychologist* 20: 125—30.

1969. *American Beliefs and Attitudes about Intelligence*. New York: Russell Sage.

Cain, Glen C. and Harold W. Watts, 1970. "Problems in Making Policy Inferences from the Coleman Report." *American Sociological Review* 35: 228—41.

Campbell, Donald T. 1969. "Reforms as Experiments." *American Psychologist* 24: 409—29.

1975. "Making the Case for Randomized Assignment to Treatments by Considering the Alternatives: Six Ways in which Quasi-Experimental Evaluations in Compensatory Education Tend to Underestimate Effects." Unpublished manuscript.

Campbell, Donald T. and Keith N. Clayton, 1961. "Avoiding Regression Effects in Panel Studies of Communication Impact." *Studies in Communication* 3: 99—118. University of Chicago, Department of Sociology.

Campbell, Donald T. and Albert Erlebacher, 1970. "How Regression Artifacts in Quasi-Experimental Evaluations Can Mistakenly Make Compensatory Education Look Harmful," in J.

Hellmuth (ed.), *The Disadvantaged Child 3: Compensatory Education: A National Debate*. New York: Brunner, Mazel.

Campbell, Donald T. and Julian L. Stanley, 1963. "Experimental and Quasi-Experimental Designs for Research on Teaching," in Nathan L. Gage (ed.), *Handbook of Research on Teaching*, 171–246. Chicago: Rand McNally.

Campbell, Ernest Q. 1969. "Adolescent Socialization," in David A. Goslin (ed.), *Handbook of Socialization Theory and Research*, chap. 20. Chicago: Rand McNally.

Chapin, F. Stuart, 1955. *Experimental Design in Sociological Research*. New York: Harper & Row.

Cicirelli, V. G. 1969. *The Impact of Head Start: An Evaluation of the Effects of Head Start on Children's Cognitive and Affective Development, 1*. Westinghouse Learning Corporation, Ohio University.

Clausen, John A. 1972. "The Life Course of Individuals," in Matilda White Riley, Marilyn Johnson and Ann Foner (eds.), *Aging and Society, 3: A Sociology of Age Stratification*, chap. 11. New York: Russell Sage.

Coleman, James S. 1970. "Reply to Cain and Watts." *American Sociological Review* 35: 242–52.

    1971. *Resources for Social Change*. New York: Wiley.

Coleman, James S., E. Q. Campbell, Carol J. Hobson, James McPartland, A. M. Mood, F. D. Weinfeld and R. L. York, 1966. *Equality of Educational Opportunity*. Washington, D.C.: U.S. Government Printing Office.

Cook, Desmond E., n.d. *The Impact of the Hawthorne Effect in Experimental Designs in Educational Research*. Columbus: Ohio State University, Final Report, Office of Education Study Project #1757.

Coward, Barbara E., J. Allen Williams, Jr. and Joe R. Feagin, 1974. "The Culture of Poverty Debate: Some Additional Data." *Social Problems* 21: 621–34.

Crain, Robert L. and Carol Sachs Weisman, 1972. *Discrimination, Personality, Achievement: A Survey of Northern Blacks*. New York: Seminar Press.

Davis, James A. 1966. "The Campus as a Frog Pond." *American Journal of Sociology* 72: 17–31.

Della Fave, L. Richard, 1974. "The Culture of Poverty Revisited: A Strategy for Research." *Social Problems* 21: 609–21.

Deutsch, Martin, 1965. "Social Intervention and the Malleability of the Child." Fourth Annual School of Education Lecture, Cornell University.

Deutsch, Martin, Irwin Katz and Arthur R. Jensen (eds.), 1968. *Social Class, Race, and Psychological Development*. New York: Holt, Rinehart and Winston.

Dobzhansky, Theodosius, 1973. *Genetic Diversity and Human Equality*. New York: Basic Books.

Drabek, Thomas and Eugene Haas, 1967. "Realism in Laboratory Simulation: Myth or Method?" *Social Forces* 46: 337–46.

Duncan, Otis D. 1969. "Inheritance of Poverty or Inheritance of Race," in Daniel P. Moynihan (ed.), *On Understanding Poverty*, chap. 4. New York: Basic Books.

Duncan, Otis Dudley, David Featherman and Beverly Duncan, 1972. *Socioeconomic Background and Achievement*. New York: Seminar Press.

Eckland, Bruce, 1967. "Genetics and Sociology: A Reconsideration." *American Sociological Review* 32: 173–94.

Edwards, A. L. 1950. *Experimental Design in Psychological Research*. New York: Holt, Rinehart and Winston.

Edwards, Esther P. 1968. "Kindergarten is Too Late." *Saturday Review* 45 (June 15): 68ff.

Ellis, Robert A. and W. Clayton Lane, 1967. "Social Mobility and Social Isolation: A Test of Sorokin's Dissociative Hypothesis." *American Sociological Review* 32: 237–46.

Faris, Robert, 1961. "Reflections on the Ability Dimension in Human Society." *American Sociological Review* 26: 835–43.

Fisher, R. A. 1937. *The Design of Experiments* (2nd edn). Edinburgh: Oliver and Boyd.

Freedman, Ronald, 1950. "Incomplete Matching in Ex Post Facto Studies." *American Journal of Sociology* 56: 485—7.

Freedman, Ronald and Amos Hawley, 1949. "Unemployment and Migration in the Depression (1930—1935)." *Journal of the American Statistical Association* 44: 260—72.

Gage, Nathan L. (ed.), 1963. *Handbook of Research on Teaching.* Chicago: Rand McNally.

Gans, Herbert, 1963. *The Urban Villagers.* New York: Macmillan.

Goffman, Erving, 1963. *Stigma: Notes on the Management of Spoiled Identity.* New York: Prentice-Hall.

Gordon, Chad, 1971. "Social Characteristics of Early Adolescence." *Daedalus* 100: 931—60.
    1973. *Looking Ahead: Self-Conceptions, Race and Family as Determinants of Adolescent Orientation to Achievement.* Washington: American Sociological Association.

Gordon, Edmund W. 1970. "Compensatory Education: Evaluation in Perspective." *IRCD Bulletin,* 6.

Gordon, Edmund W. and Doxey A. Wilkerson, 1966. *Compensatory Education for the Disadvantaged: Programs and Practices Preschool Through College.* Princeton: College Entrance Examination Board.

Goslin, David, 1963. *The Search for Ability.* New York: Russell Sage.

Gottfried, Nathan W. 1973. "Effects of Early Intervention Programs," in Kent Miller and Ralph Dreger (eds.), *Comparative Studies of Blacks and Whites in the United States,* chap. 9. New York: Seminar Press.

Gove, Walter R. 1970. "Societal Reaction as an Explanation of Mental Illness: An Evaluation." *American Sociological Review* 35: 873—84.

Graves, Theodore D. 1974. "Urban Indian Personality and the 'Culture of Poverty.'" *American Ethnologist* 1: 65—86.

Greeley, Andrew M. 1974. *Ethnicity in the United States: A Preliminary Reconnaissance.* New York: Wiley.

Greenwood, Ernest, 1945. *Experimental Sociology, A Study in Method.* New York: Crown.

Hagan, John, 1973. "Labelling and Deviance: A Case Study in the Sociology of the Interesting." *Social Problems* 20: 447—58.

Han, Wan Sang, 1969. "Two Conflicting Theses: Common Values Versus Class Differential Values." *American Sociological Review* 34: 679—90.

Hargreaves, David, 1967. *Social Relations in a Secondary School.* New York: Humanities Press.

Harmon, Harry H. 1967. *Modern Factor Analysis.* University of Chicago Press.

Harrington, Michael, 1962. *The Other America: Poverty in the United States.* New York: Macmillan.

Hauser, Robert M. 1972. *Socioeconomic Background and Educational Performance.* Washington: American Sociological Association.

Hellmuth, Jerome (ed.), 1970. *The Disadvantaged Child. 3: Compensatory Education: A National Debate.* New York: Brunner, Mazel.

Herrnstein, Richard J. 1971. "I.Q." *The Atlantic* 228: 44—64.

Hunt, David E. and Robert H. Hardt, 1969. "The Effect of Upward Bound Programs on the Attitudes, Motivation, and Academic Achievement of Negro Students." *Journal of Social Issues* 25: 117—29.

Hunt, J. McV. 1961. *Intelligence and Experience.* New York: Ronald.
    1969. "Has Compensatory Education Failed?" *Harvard Educational Review* 39: 278—300.

Ikeda, Kiyoshi, Frank Laycock and J. Milton Yinger, 1972. "A Seven-Year Program to Prepare Talented Youths for College." *The Urban Review* 5: 41—5.

Ikeda, Kiyoshi, J. Milton Yinger and Frank Laycock, 1970. "Reforms as Experiments and Experiments as Reforms." Unpublished Manuscript. Oberlin College, Oberlin, Ohio.

Jencks, Christopher, Marshall Smith, Henry Acland, Mary Jo Bane, David Cohen, Herbert Gintis, Barbara Heyns and Stephen Michelson, 1972. *Inequality: A Reassessment of the Effect of Family and Schooling in America.* New York: Basic Books.

Jensen, Arthur R. 1969. "How Much Can We Boost IQ and Scholastic Achievement?" *Harvard Educational Review* 39: 1—123.

Jung, J. 1971. *The Experimenter's Dilemma*. New York: Harper & Row.

Kagan, Jerome, 1971. "A Conception of Early Adolescence." *Daedalus* 100: 997—1012.

Kallen, David J. (ed.), 1973. *Nutrition, Development, and Social Behavior*. Washington: National Institues of Health, U.S. Department of Health, Education, and Welfare.

Kanter, Rosabeth Moss, 1972. *Commitment and Community: Communes and Utopias in Sociological Perspective*. Cambridge: Harvard University Press.

Labov, William, 1972. *Language in the Inner City: Studies in the Black English Vernacular*. Philadelphia: University of Pennsylvania Press.

Larson, Meredith A. and Freya E. Dittmann, 1975. *Compensatory Education and Early Adolescence: Reviewing our National Strategy*. Menlo Park, California: Stanford Research Institute.

Lemert, Edwin, 1972. *Human Deviance* (2nd edn). New York: Prentice-Hall.

Lempert, Richard O. 1966. "Strategies in Research Design in Legal Impact Studies." *Sociology of Law* 6: 1—19.

Lewis, Oscar, 1959. *Five Families: Mexican Case Studies in the Culture of Poverty*. New York: Basic Books.

   1961. *The Children of Sanchez*. New York: Random House.

   1966. *La Vida: A Puerto Rican Family in the Culture of Poverty*. New York: Random House.

   1966a. "The Culture of Poverty." *Scientific American* 215: 19—25.

Liebow, Elliot, 1967. *Tally's Corner: A Study of Negro Streetcorner Men*. Boston: Little Brown.

Lorenz, Konrad, 1960. *On Aggression*. New York: Harcourt Brace Jovanovich.

Matza, David and Gresham Sykes, 1961. "Juvenile Delinquency and Subterranean Values." *American Sociological Review* 26: 712—19.

Mead, Margaret, Theodosius Dobzhansky, Ethel Tobach and Robert Light (eds.), 1968. *Science and the Concept of Race*. New York: Columbia University Press.

Mercer, Jane R., 1971. *Labelling the Mentally Retarded*. Berkeley: University of California Press.

Meyer, John W. 1970. "High School Effects on College Intentions." *American Journal of Sociology* 76: 59—70.

Miller, Kent S. and Ralph M. Dreger, 1973. *Comparative Studies of Blacks and Whites in the United States*. New York: Seminar Press.

Miller, Walter B. 1958. "Lower Class Culture as a Generating Milieu of Gang Delinquency." *Journal of Social Issues* 14: 5—19.

Montagu, Ashley, 1972. *Man and Aggression* (2nd edn). New York: Oxford University Press.

   1972a."Sociogenic Brain Damage." *American Anthropologist* 74: 1045—61.

Newell, Peter, 1970. "Jensen Defends His Views on Race, Class and Intelligence." London: *Times Educational Supplement* (July 24): 9.

Panos, Robert J. 1973. "Picking Winners or Developing Potential." *School Review* 81: 437—50.

Parker, Seymour and Robert J. Kleiner, 1970. "The Culture of Poverty: An Adjustive Dimension." *American Anthropologist* 72: 516—27.

Porter, James N. 1974. "Race, Socialization, and Early Occupational Attainment." *American Sociological Review* 39: 303—16.

Rainwater, Lee, 1970. *Behind Ghetto Walls*. Chicago: Aldine.

   1970a. "The Problem of Lower Class Culture." *Journal of Social Issues* 26: 133—48.

Rehberg, Richard A., Walter E. Schafer and Judie Sinclair, 1970. "Toward a Temporal Sequence of Adolescent Achievement Variables." *American Sociological Review* 35: 34—48.

Riley, Matilda W. 1963. *Sociological Research*. New York: Harcourt Brace Jovanovich.

Roach, Jack and Orville Gursslin, 1967. "An Evaluation of the Concept 'Culture of Poverty.'" *Social Forces* 45: 383—92.

Roberts, S.O. and Carell P. Horton, 1973. "Extent of and Effects of Desegregation," in Kent Miller and Ralph Dreger (eds.), *Comparative Studies of Blacks and Whites in the United States*, chap. 10. New York: Seminar Press.

Rockefeller Panel Reports, 1961. *Prospect for America*. New York: Doubleday.

Rodman, Hyman, 1963. "The Lower Class Value Stretch." *Social Forces* 42: 205–15.

Rosenthal, Robert and Lenore Jacobson, 1968. *Pygmalion in the Classroom*. New York: Holt, Rinehart and Winston.

Rummel, R. J. 1967. "Understanding Factor Analysis." *Journal of Conflict Resolution* 12: 444–80.

St. John, Nancy and Ralph Lewis, 1971. "The Influence of School Racial Context on Academic Achievement." *Social Forces* 49: 68–79.

Samuda, Ronald J. 1973. "Racial Discrimination Through Mental Testing." *IRCD Bulletin* (May).

Scheff, Thomas, 1974. "The Labelling Theory of Mental Illness." *American Sociological Review* 39: 444–52.

Schervish, Paul G. 1973. "The Labeling Perspective: Its Bias and Potential in the Study of Political Deviance." *American Sociologist* 8: 47–57.

Schur, Edwin M. 1971. *Labelling Deviant Behavior*. New York: Harper & Row.

Schwitzgebel, Ralph, 1964. *Streetcorner Research*. Cambridge: Harvard University Press.

Selltiz, Claire, Marie Jahoda, Morton Deutsch and Stuart W. Cook, 1959. *Research Methods in Social Relations* (rev. edn). New York: Holt, Rinehart and Winston.

Sewell, William H., 1967. "Review of the Coleman Report." *American Sociological Review* 32: 475–9.

Sewell, William H., A. O. Haller and Alejandro Portes, 1969: "The Educational and Early Occupational Attainment Process." *American Sociological Review* 34: 82–92.

    1971. "Inequality of Opportunity for Higher Education." *American Sociological Review* 36: 793-809.

Sewell, William H. and Vimal P. Shah, 1967. "Socioeconomic Status, Intelligence, and the Attainment of Higher Education." *Sociology of Education* 39: 1–23.

    1968. "Social Class, Parental Encouragement, and Educational Aspirations." *American Journal of Sociology* 73: 559–72.

Simpson, George E. and J. Milton Yinger, 1972. *Racial and Cultural Minorities* (4th edn). New York: Harper & Row.

Smith, Marshall S. and Joan S. Bissel, 1970. "Report Analysis: The Impact of Head Start." *Harvard Educational Review* 40: 51–104.

Smith, Robert B. 1972. "Neighborhood Context and College Plans: An Ordinal Path Analysis." *Social Forces* 51: 199–217.

Stanley, Julian C., 1973. *Compensatory Education for Children, Ages 2–8*. Baltimore: Johns Hopkins University Press.

Stanley, Julian and John R. Hills, 1970. "Easier Test Improves Prediction of Black Students' College Grades." *Journal of Negro Education* 39: 390.

Stephenson, R. N. 1957. "Mobility Orientation and Stratification of 1,000 Ninth Graders." *American Sociological Review* 22: 204–12.

Summers, Anita A. and Barbara L. Wolfe, 1975. "Which School Resources Help Learning? Efficiency and Equity in Philadelphia Public Schools." *Business Review*: 4–28. Philadelphia: The Federal Reserve Bank of Philadelphia.

Svensson, Allan, 1971. *Relative Achievement: School Performance in Relation to Intelligence, Sex and Home Environment*. Stockholm: Almquist and Wiksell.

Turner, Ralph H. 1964. *The Social Context of Ambition*. San Francisco: Chandler.

    1972. "Deviance Avowal as Neutralization of Commitment." *Social Problems* 19: 308–21.

Tyler, Leona, 1965. *The Psychology of Human Differences* (3rd edn). New York: Prentice-Hall.

United States Department of Commerce, Bureau of the Census, 1973. *The Social and Economic Status of the Black Population in the United States.* Washington: U.S. Government Printing Office.

Valentine, Charles, 1968. *Culture and Poverty.* University of Chicago Press.

van den Berghe, Pierre L. 1974. "Bringing Beasts Back In: Toward a Biosocial Theory of Aggression." *American Sociological Review* 39: 777–88.

Vernon, Philip E. 1969. *Intelligence and Cultural Environment.* London: Methuen.

Warner, W. Lloyd, 1944. *Who Shall be Educated?* New York: Harper & Row.

Welty, Gordon A. 1969. *The Logic of Evaluation.* Washington: Educational Resources Institute.

Williams, Robin M. Jr. 1958. "Continuity and Change in Sociological Study." *American Sociological Review* 23: 622–3.

Wilson, Alan B. 1969. *The Consequences of Segregation: Academic Achievement in a Northern Community.* Berkeley: Glendessary Press.

Yinger, J. Milton, 1965. *Toward a Field Theory of Behavior.* New York: McGraw-Hill.

Yinger, J. Milton, Kiyoshi Ikeda and Frank Laycock, 1967. "Treating Matching as a Variable in a Sociological Experiment." *American Sociological Review* 32: 801–12.

Index

131